THE YOUNG RUNNER'S GUIDE TO NUTRITION

THE YOUNG RUNNER'S GUIDE TO NUTRITION

HOW TO FUEL YOUR BODY TO TRAIN SMARTER, RUN FASTER, AND RECOVER QUICKER

MICHELE PETTINGER

RRCA LEVEL II RUN COACH, CFNC

Published by:

an imprint of Ulysses Press
PO Box 3440
Berkeley, CA 94703
www.velopress.com

VeloPress is the leading publisher of books on sports for passionate and dedicated athletes around the world. Focused on cycling, triathlon, running, swimming, nutrition/diet, and more, VeloPress books help you achieve your goals and reach the top of your game.

ISBN: 978-1-64604-777-2
Library of Congress Control Number: 2024945011

Printed in Canada
10 9 8 7 6 5 4 3 2 1

Project editor: Kierra Sondereker
Managing editor: Claire Chun
Editor: Mary Calvez
Proofreader: Janet Vail
Front cover design: Akangksha Sarmah
Artwork: cover illustrations from Freepik; interior illustrations from shutterstock.com—chapter openers and pages 26, 29 © VectorMine; sun for charts © jayaZgraphics; page 8 suma2020; page 9 © Nina Piankova; page 15 © Ansty; page 20 © CoolRaccoon; page 31 © Anastasiia Usenko; page 34 © Taash; page 40 © Tartila
Interior design: Winnie Liu
Production: Jake Flaherty Design

In loving memory of my parents, Al and Clarine Abramowitz.

To my dad, Al, whose passion for coaching and devotion to young runners left a lasting legacy.

To my mom, Clarine, whose quiet strength and unwavering belief in me continue to guide my path.

CONTENTS

INTRODUCTION

It was a warm summer evening in 1982. I was 12. The Midwest air smelled of corn fields and fresh-cut grass. I looked down at my new ASICS Tigers as I laced them up, sitting on the cement stairs that led up to my home, excited, but nervous all at once. I could hear my parents whispering—my mom telling my dad to take it easy. He was taking me on my first run. One mile, to the stop sign and back. Little did I know that this run would start the growth of a passion for a sport that would ultimately guide me through life, giving me a lens through which to view the world and a profession that continues to feed my soul.

My life is woven with threads of running memories like these. My heartfelt intention is for you to embrace the freedom of running and through nutrition education enable you to unlock your fullest potential both now and in the years to come. Running is not just a sport; it's a lifestyle that can change your life.

Your adolescent years are pivotal, a window of opportunity to embark on the journey of self-discovery and lay the foundation for the future. When I was growing up, nutrition was not at the forefront of conversation at practice or races. But we now have science to show us how nutrition strategies can improve our performance on and off the track.

Still, the internet and social media are filled with articles on runners with disordered eating and stress fractures, or runners who don't believe in themselves. You may even think you must look a certain way to be a strong runner. Your body composition will change over the years, and you are at a unique time of life that can seem overwhelming, but you do have a say in how you move through it. And I want to foster your autonomy in making decisions about your unique physiology.

Coaches, you have a tremendous job. Our role as a mentor to these young runners is a gift and a challenge to bring them up in a program that fosters their love for the sport. Your school most likely does not have a sports dietitian, nor do you have the funds to hire one to talk to the team. This book is also for you. It provides insights into young runners' nutritional needs, training strategies, and, most importantly, how to foster a healthy relationship with the sport. Your influence is invaluable, and I would love for you to share the principles and tools laid out here with your team.

Parents and guardians, I haven't been in your exact shoes, but I've shared the landscape. You're working in and out of the home. You may be managing your sport and getting your children to theirs. And with practice times, it may happen in shifts. When is there time to cook? This book is also for you. It has tips on meal prepping, how to talk with your young runner about nutrition, how to get involved together, and sample weekly plans based on the recipes in the book.

My hope is that we don't see a growth in articles written about low energy availability in youth running or runners struggling with body image. Instead, we are reading articles about the introduction of nutrition education at the grassroots level and other training protocols, like proper recovery and sleep, resulting in outstanding high school performances.

Thank you for exploring these pages. I would love to hear from you. I'm in your corner and rooting for you! Please feel free to contact me with any questions or concerns. I'm here to support you on your journey.

Keep running,
Coach Michele

CHAPTER ONE

NAVIGATING ADOLESCENCE: UNDERSTANDING YOUR PHYSIOLOGY

Adolescence is a new birth, for the higher and more completely human traits are now born.

—G. Stanley Hall

I was standing at the start line of my high school track. In my 15-year-old mind, everyone in the stadium was looking at me. I thought they could see right through how uncomfortable I felt in my body. I was unsure how it would move through space that day. Would it flow, or would it feel out of sync—like my arms and legs were not working together? I wasn't thinking about whether or not my hormones—the signals in the body that regulate our energy, support bone growth, and promote muscle repair—were in balance. And I certainly wasn't thinking about how my nutrition could impact my hormones, growth and development, or performance on the track.

Since my days on the high school track and cross-country course, there has been tremendous growth in sports nutrition. We now have science to show us how nutrition strategies can improve our performance on and off the track. I'm excited to share with you information that will give you a step up in building a strong foundation for your running career.

During adolescence, your body undergoes a series of changes that can seem overwhelming. However, understanding these changes is the first step toward learning how to navigate them. These physiological changes impact bone health, muscle growth, hormonal shifts, and brain and cognitive development. And they all play a role in your running performance. Let's break it down, step by step, and explore how each factor can impact your running.

Picture your body as a one-of-a-kind house custom-built to your unique physiology. The house is made of various materials, like a concrete foundation, wood framing, electrical, and plumbing. All systems are in place to ensure structural integrity as the house ages. Similarly, your bones are the foundation of your body, essential to the inner workings. Your muscles are dynamic, like the framing that provides strength and movement. Your brain acts as the intelligent control system overseeing various bodily functions, but closely linked to it are your hormones, which operate much like a thermostat, regulating and fine-tuning your body's internal environment.

START WITH THESE NUTRITION BASICS[1]

- **Limit caffeine, sugar, and processed foods:** Reduce consumption of sugary and caffeinated drinks, snacks, and processed foods. These can negatively affect energy levels and overall health. Read about the negative effects of energy drinks on page 48.
- **Pay attention to proper hydration:** Drink enough water throughout the day and before, during, and after exercise. Learn more about proper hydration on page 39.
- **Eat a balanced diet of whole foods:** Fruits, vegetables, whole grains, and healthy fats provide essential nutrients for sustained energy, faster recovery, and improved overall health.

BONE HEALTH

Your bones are your foundation. The strength of your bones is essential to your overall health and well-being long into adulthood. I remember when I was younger thinking life would be over at 50, but I'm well into my 50s and still running and competing in races. Some of my best running years were in my 40s. I understand that right now, you are probably not thinking past your next race, or how you will find time to study for calculus, or whether or not your parents will let you go out on Friday night, but your bone development is a big deal—the

1 Christian Hecht et al., "Nutritional Recommendations for the Young Athlete: Current Concept Review," *Journal of the Pediatric Orthopaedic Society of North America* 5, no. 1 (February 1, 2023), https://doi.org/10.55275/JPOSNA-2023-599.

choices you make now in training, nutrition, and recovery practices like sleep will impact the future health of your bones.

Your bones are primarily made up of the minerals calcium and phosphorus. The density of those minerals is known as bone mineral density (BMD). The higher the BMD, the stronger your bones. Scientific research reveals that we accumulate nearly 90 percent of our total bone mass during adolescence.[2]

A process is happening in the background to do this. It's called bone remodeling. Just like your house requires maintenance and occasional remodeling, our bones undergo a similar process. Cells called osteoclasts are continually breaking down old bone, while others called osteoblasts are working to build new bone tissue. This remodeling process directly impacts BMD by balancing bone breakdown and formation. If the breakdown happens faster than the rebuilding, then your BMD decreases. The less dense your bones, the more susceptible they are to injury. For example, if your bones are not getting the nutrients they need or you are not recovering enough from running, your bones will struggle to rebuild.

2 Sale, Craig, and Kirsty Jayne Elliott-Sale. "Nutrition and Athlete Bone Health." Sports Medicine 49, no. 2 (November 6, 2019): 139–51. https://doi.org/10.1007/s40279-019-01161-2.

Research has shown that youth runners, particularly girls, are at risk for bone stress injury. This is "evidenced by cross country runners experiencing the first (girls) and third (boys) highest rates of bone stress injury ... among US high school athletes."[3] In this context, nutrition plays a crucial role. Think of it as fuel for your body—you need enough energy and the right minerals to keep your bones healthy and strong.

Super Foods for Strong Bones

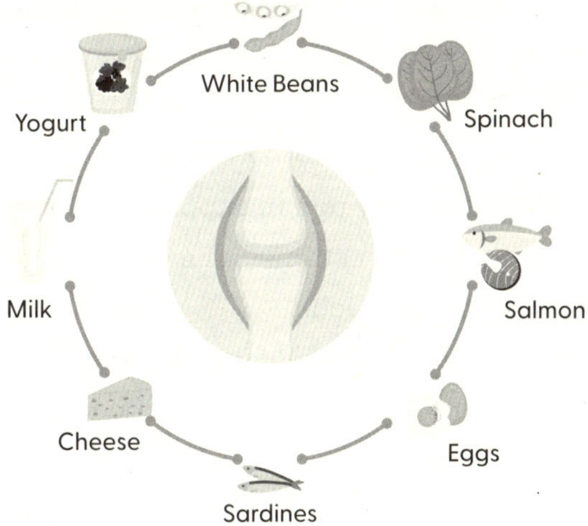

In a comprehensive review of scientific studies from 2023, researchers found that vitamin D deficiency and the female and male athlete triads—a set of three interrelated conditions that can affect both female and male athletes—can profoundly impact bone health.[4] For more details on vitamin D, turn to

3 Brian J. Krabak et al., "Youth Running Consensus Statement: Minimising Risk of Injury and Illness in Youth Runners," *British Journal of Sports Medicine* 55, no. 6 (October 29, 2020): 305–18, https://doi.org/10.1136/bjsports-2020-102518.

4 Aubrey Armento et al., "Bone Health in Young Athletes: A Narrative Review of the Recent Literature," *Current Osteoporosis Reports* 21, no. 4 (June 8, 2023): 447–58, https://doi.org/10.1007/s11914-023-00796-5.

chapter 2. Chapter 4 discusses the athlete triads, their effects, and, most importantly, how to prevent them.

WHAT IS THE DIFFERENCE BETWEEN A STRESS FRACTURE AND A BONE STRESS INJURY?

You've most likely heard the term stress fracture. Recently, the term bone stress injury (BSI) has become more popular, as many BSIs do not have a discernible fracture line. BSIs "occur when excessive repetitive stress is applied to normal bone, resulting in structural bone weakness and pain." [5] Stress fractures are a type of BSI with a discernible fracture line on imaging.

Nutrients that play a key role in supporting bone health:

- → **Calcium.** Essential for strong bones. Sources: milk, yogurt, cheese, kale, and spinach.
- → **Vitamin D.** Helps absorb calcium. Sources: sunlight, fatty fish (like salmon), egg yolks, and fortified foods (milk, cereal).
- → **Protein.** Builds bones. Sources: lean meats, poultry, fish, eggs, beans, nuts, and seeds.
- → **Omega-3 Fatty Acids.** Have anti-inflammatory properties and support bone health. They are found in fatty fish, flaxseeds, chia seeds, and walnuts.
- → **Magnesium.** Supports bone remodeling. Sources: seeds, whole grains, leafy greens, and legumes.

5 Armento et al., "Bone Health in Young Athletes."

- **Vitamin K.** Necessary for bone mineralization and calcium regulation. Sources: leafy greens like kale, spinach, broccoli, and Brussels sprouts.

Recipes in chapter 7 to support bone health: Blueberry Peach Yogurt Smoothie, Teriyaki Salmon Bowl with Crunchy Asian Slaw, and Fudgy Chocolate Chia Pudding.

MUSCLE DEVELOPMENT

Your muscles are like the framing of your house. They support the foundation by evenly distributing loads from the structure's weight and external forces throughout the foundation. Your muscles also support the movement of your bones by contracting and controlling dynamic movements like flexion and extension. For example, in your running gait cycle, your leg drives forward, flexing at the hip and knee to then make contact with the ground and extend backward.

During puberty, the rate of muscle development between boys and girls shifts, leading to unique changes in each gender. Let's examine these changes in more detail.

MUSCLE DEVELOPMENT IN THE YOUNG FEMALE RUNNER

During puberty, girls experience changes in muscle development influenced by hormonal changes. Your estrogen levels begin to increase. Your growth slows, and there is a smaller increase in muscle mass. Your body starts to change shape, and fat mass increases; these natural changes are part of your body's preparation for the reproductive years. These changes are natural and a part of your journey.[6]

MUSCLE DEVELOPMENT IN THE YOUNG MALE RUNNER

Hormones also drive changes in muscle development for boys. During puberty, boys experience a surge in testosterone production. Testosterone regulates increased muscle mass and strength by stimulating growth hormone production, increasing the number of muscle cells and enhancing their ability to contract, which could directly contribute to improved running performance. Some boys will experience more significant gains than others, likely due to genetics, training, and nutrition.[7]

NUTRIENTS TO SUPPORT YOUR MUSCLE DEVELOPMENT

Muscles are a source of power, and they need the right fuel at the right time to function optimally. Chapter 2 delves into the crucial role of protein in muscle repair and growth, while chapter 3 unveils the secret of timing your fuel to maximize recovery. By understanding and implementing these principles, you can take control of your muscle development, repair, and recovery.

---

6 Espen Tønnessen et al., "Performance Development in Adolescent Track and Field Athletes according to Age, Sex and Sport Discipline," ed. Nir Eynon, *PLOS ONE* 10, no. 6 (June 4, 2015): e0129014, https://doi.org/10.1371/journal.pone.0129014.

7 Tønnessen et al., "Performance Development."

Macronutrients:

- **Carbohydrates:** Provide energy for workouts and muscle building. Complex carbohydrate sources: whole grains, fruits, and vegetables. Simple carbohydrate sources: dried fruit, granola, pretzels, fruit, sports drinks, energy chews, or gels.
- **Protein:** Helps muscles repair and grow. Sources: lean meats, poultry, fish, eggs, beans, nuts, and seeds.
- **Healthy Fats:** Support hormone production for muscle growth. Sources: fatty fish, flaxseeds, chia seeds, and nuts.

Micronutrients:

- **Vitamins and minerals:** The three micronutrients that are essential for muscle function and recovery in young runners—iron, calcium, and vitamin D. Sources: fatty fish, dairy products, nuts, seeds, leafy greens, and bananas.

Recipes in chapter 7 to support muscle health: Chocolate Cherry Recovery Smoothie, Quinoa with Sweet Potato and Fried Eggs, and Power Breakfast Cookies.

OTHER FACTORS THAT WILL IMPACT YOUR HORMONES, BONE HEALTH, MUSCLE DEVELOPMENT, AND BRAIN AND COGNITIVE FUNCTION

Genetics—Genetics is the science of genes and how traits are passed on from generation to generation. For example, you may have a higher proportion of fast-twitch muscle fibers responsible for quick, explosive movements like sprinting. In contrast, your teammate may have more slow-twitch fibers that are better suited for endurance activities like distance running.

Sleep—Studies have shown that sleep deprivation in adolescent athletes is associated with an increased risk of musculoskeletal injury and a decline in cognitive performance. The recommended minimum amount of sleep for individuals between the ages of 7 and 19 is 8 to 9 hours per night.[8]

Training Load—Scientists believe that manipulating the mode, duration, and intensity of exercise could help improve bone health.[9] While I acknowledge that you are operating under the guidance of a coach, I strongly encourage you to initiate a respectful dialogue with your coach if you feel that your body is not keeping up with the demands of the training. Your physical well-being is a shared responsibility, and open communication is key. See chapter 4 for signs that you may be under-fueled and over-trained.

BRAIN AND COGNITIVE DEVELOPMENT

Consider this: Just as you engage in physical exercises to strengthen your bones and muscles, you can also engage in activities that boost your brain's cognitive development. Much like your home's intelligent control system, your brain constantly receives messaging that allows it to refine, grow, and

8 Rachel A. Coel et al., "Sleep and the Young Athlete," *Sports Health: A Multidisciplinary Approach* 15, no. 4 (July 19, 2022): 194173812211087, https://doi.org/10.1177/19417381221108732.

9 Aubrey Armento et al., "Bone Health in Young Athletes: A Narrative Review of the Recent Literature." *Current Osteoporosis Reports* 21, no. 4 (June 8, 2023): 447–58. https://doi.org/10.1007/s11914-023-00796-5.

mature. This process, known as neuroplasticity, can be positively influenced by running. Studies have shown that engaging in exercises like running can substantially improve attention, memory, and executive function skills such as planning and problem-solving.[10] These are all functions you actively use when running! For example, paying attention and staying focused during a workout, building muscle memory, and making decisions within a race.

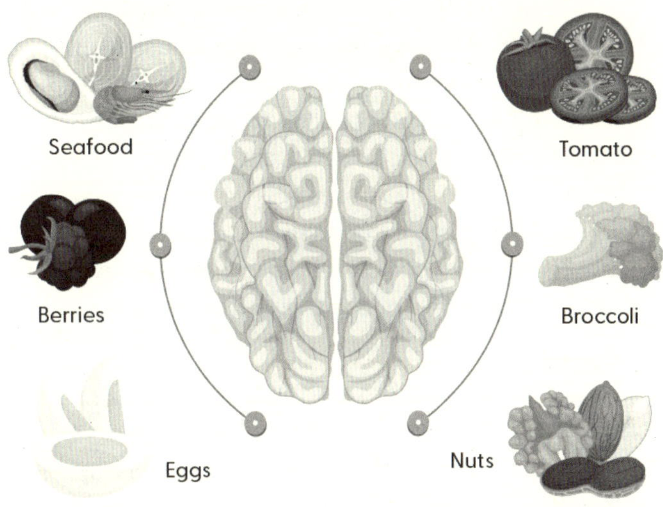

And you guessed it! Your brain needs to be adequately fueled to have the nutrients it needs to process and adapt to these inputs. You will learn more about hormones in the next section, but it's important to note here that estrogen and testosterone play important roles in brain development. Insufficient fueling

10 Laura Mandolesi et al., "Effects of Physical Exercise on Cognitive Functioning and Wellbeing: Biological and Psychological Benefits," *Frontiers in Psychology* 9, no. 9 (April 27, 2018), https://doi.org/10.3389/fpsyg.2018.00509.

may affect hormone production, leading to imbalances that can impact brain growth and neural connections.

CHARLIE'S STORY

I began running with my local running club in middle school. I was a natural, the coach said, and I progressed quickly to being one of the top runners. When I entered high school, I was excited to be a top runner on the team. Summer practices went well, and I bonded with my new team. However, once school started, my high school schedule was more demanding of my time, and I had more extracurricular activities outside of running. I struggled at practices to keep up with the others, and I was not performing in races. I was struggling in the classroom, too. My top 7 position on the team was in jeopardy. I was not only physically exhausted but mentally drained as well. What was happening? My coaches seemed to dismiss it, saying that it might just be a phase; they did ask me if I was getting enough sleep, which, admittedly, I wasn't.

Because I struggled in school, I took my lunch break in the study hall, grabbed what I could from the grab-and-go in the cafeteria, and tried to catch up. I started coming home from practice so tired that all I wanted to do was go to bed, even skipping dinner, only to toss and turn all night, unable to settle into deep sleep. Then, one day, I made it to have lunch at the cafeteria with my teammates, and I noticed a handful of them with their lunches from home—Tupperware filled with meat and rice and vegetables, salads, and hearty sandwiches. I asked one of my teammates if they ate like that every day. And he said, "I have to. I wouldn't be able to run if I didn't." I looked down at my fruit and chips, and I realized how little I was eating in comparison. It wasn't for lack of wanting to; it just hadn't struck me as a priority. So, I started to pay attention and ask questions. Did they eat before practice? What did they eat for dinner?

Thankfully, I could talk with my mom about it, and she said she would help me get the right foods at the right time. We began to work on it together. She researched and prepared nutritious meals for me, and we discussed the importance of nutrition timing. Her support and guidance were instrumental in my journey. I've learned so much, and my running turned around. I started to feel like running again. Just by eating a lot! Schoolwork got more manageable, and I was no longer getting recurring colds.

See chapter 6 for ideas for supporting your family's unique demands, including tips for meal planning, food preparation, and fostering open communication around nutrition.

Boost your brain power with these nutrients:

- **Omega-3 Fatty Acids.** Help with memory, learning, and thinking. Sources: fatty fish, flaxseeds, chia seeds, and walnuts. Omega-3s are good for your brain.
- **Balanced Blood Sugar Levels.** Eating meals and snacks with a mix of carbohydrates, protein, and healthy fats keeps your blood sugar steady. This gives your brain a steady supply of energy. You can learn more about nutrition timing in chapter 3.
- **Micronutrients.** Vitamin E, vitamin B12, folate, and iron are some of the vitamins and minerals important for brain

power. Sources: fruits, vegetables, whole grains, and lean proteins.

Recipes in chapter 7 to support brain and cognitive development: Berry Power Smoothie, Sardine Toast, and Quinoa and Sweet Potato Power Salad.

HORMONE HEALTH

Hormones, like chemical messengers, are produced by glands in our bodies and released into the bloodstream to regulate various bodily functions.[11] If your hormones are out of balance, it can affect your bone health, muscle development, and brain and cognitive function and it's time to take special care to consider the specific needs of your gender. Just like a malfunctioning thermometer in your house, if it's broken, your home won't know when to heat or cool, making the living environment uncomfortable. But don't worry; you can assist your hormones in regulating them through proper nutrition!

HORMONES AND THE YOUNG FEMALE RUNNER

I remember so many uncomfortable times in the classroom and at practices. My periods were painful and disruptive to my adolescent life. But remember, these changes are normal and part of your journey. Your hips widen, your breasts develop, and your body hair grows. You might feel bloated, irritable, and unmotivated to complete the workout at practice. These

---

11 Marci A. Goolsby and Nicole Boniquit, "Bone Health in Athletes," *Sports Health: A Multidisciplinary Approach* 9, no. 2 (November 30, 2016): 108–17, https://doi.org/10.1177/1941738116677732.

hormonal fluctuations are unique to this stage of life, but hormones continue to be a factor as you age. Let's try to understand what is happening now so you can gather the tools for navigating these changes to help you feel in control of making it through this stage and future stages with more ease.

Let's explore the primary female growth and sex hormones: estrogen, progesterone, and small amounts of testosterone. Estrogen promotes bone health, regulates menstruation, and affects muscle growth. Progesterone balances estrogen, prepares the body for pregnancy, and regulates menstruation. Testosterone contributes to muscle development and strength.[12]

If hormones become unbalanced, you can stop having your period. This is known as amenorrhea, part of the female athlete triad (see page 79). Several factors can lead to the loss of your period, such as inadequate fueling or overtraining. If your hormones are not in balance, it can lead to a decrease in BMD (remember that from the Bone Health section?), and low BMD increases the chance of a stress fracture and long-term bone health issues. Other factors might include a medical condition or medications like birth control.[13] If you lose your period, please seek the advice of a medical professional. It is essential not to ignore it, as it can affect your long-term reproductive health, bone, and cardiovascular health.

Your menstrual cycle can affect performance in various ways. For example, low iron due to blood loss can impact your

---

12 Goolsby and Boniquit, "Bone Health in Athletes."

13 Goolsby and Boniquit, "Bone Health in Athletes."

endurance capacity and aerobic adaptation.[14] Blood loss can also contribute to lower energy availability and a condition called relative energy deficiency in sports (REDs).[15] You will read more about these nutrition challenges in chapter 4.

In addition to drinking plenty of water to help with bloating and other symptoms, dietitians are starting to explore nutritional strategies you can implement at each stage of your menstrual cycle to aid with the hormone fluctuations that can affect your mood, energy, and sleep.[16]

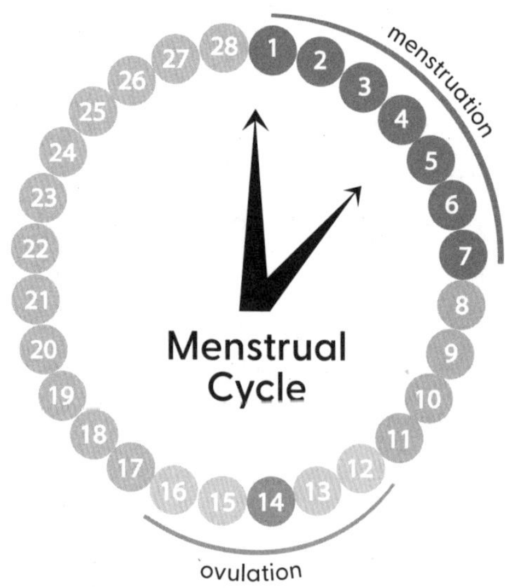

14 Ben Desbrow, "Youth Athlete Development and Nutrition," *Sports Medicine* 51, no. 1 (September 13, 2021), https://doi.org/10.1007/s40279-021-01534-6.

15 Craig Sale and Kirsty Jayne Elliott-Sale, "Nutrition and Athlete Bone Health," *Sports Medicine* 49, no. 2 (November 6, 2019): 139–51, https://doi.org/10.1007/s40279-019-01161-2.

16 Maki Yazawa, "A Dietitian on the '4 Seasons' to Know for Cycle Syncing," Well+Good (Well+Good, April 27, 2024), https://www.wellandgood.com/menstrual-cycle-foods.

MENSTRUAL PHASE (DAYS 1–5)

Iron-rich foods are important for replacing iron lost during menstruation.[17] Sources: lean meats, fish, beans, lentils, tofu, spinach, and fortified cereals.

Include vitamin C-rich foods to help you absorb iron. Sources: citrus fruits, strawberries, bell peppers, and broccoli.

Recipes: Tofu Poké Bowl with Spicy Mayo, Sheet Pan Greek Turkey Meatballs and Vegetables with Lemony Rice, and Strawberry Spinach Salad with Goat Cheese.

FOLLICULAR PHASE (DAYS 5–14)

Your estrogen levels are increasing, and your energy is returning. To support your energy levels, focus on balanced meals of complex carbohydrates, lean proteins, and healthy fats.

Help reduce inflammation with foods rich in omega-3 fatty acids, such as fatty fish, flaxseeds, chia seeds, and walnuts.

Recipes: Waffle Breakfast Sandwich, Chicken Caesar Wrap, and Fish Burrito with Creole Seasoning.

OVULATORY PHASE (DAYS 14–16)

Your estrogen levels are now at their peak, and you will most likely experience a performance improvement. Consume foods that provide easily accessible energy. Sources: whole grains and lean proteins.

Consume antioxidant-rich foods, such as berries, dark chocolate, spinach, and kale, to continue to help with inflammation.

Recipes: Homemade Granola and Yogurt Bowl, Apple-Almond Chicken Salad, Almond Butter Banana Bread with Chocolate Chips and Walnuts.

---

17 Desbrow, "Youth Athlete Development and Nutrition."

LUTEAL PHASE (DAYS 16–28)

During this premenstrual phase, progesterone levels rise, which may increase cravings for carbohydrates and sweets. Choose complex carbohydrates, such as whole grains, fruits, and vegetables, to help stabilize blood sugar levels and satisfy cravings.

To alleviate bloating and mood swings, include foods rich in magnesium. Sources: nuts, seeds, whole grains, leafy greens, and legumes.

Recipes: Maple Banana Custard Oatmeal, White Bean and Avocado Wrap with Chipotle Slaw, Chana "Chickpea" Masala.

HORMONES AND THE YOUNG MALE RUNNER

For male runners, testosterone is a pivotal hormone. It's responsible for the changes you experience during puberty, such as hair growth, a deeper voice, and increased muscle mass. Physical exercise can temporarily boost testosterone levels, aiding in muscle building and repair. However, a lack of proper nutrition, rest, and recovery can lead to a decrease in testosterone levels, reducing muscle mass, strength, and overall performance. This can affect your agility, speed, and power, and increase the risk of bone stress injuries.

Low testosterone levels can negatively affect physical performance and mood, mental health, and motivation. They can also contribute to low energy availability, a component of the male athlete triad. If you think you may have a hormonal imbalance, it is best to consult with a healthcare professional, such as your doctor or a registered sports dietitian, to discuss your concerns. For more information on managing these challenges, please read chapter 4.

Nutrients to help support testosterone levels:

- → **Cholesterol.** Testosterone is made from cholesterol, so it's okay to eat foods that have it to support testosterone production. Sources: Eggs, cheese, and shellfish.
- → **Zinc.** Zinc is essential for testosterone production and reproductive health. Sources: Red meat, poultry, beans, nuts, and whole grains.
- → **Vitamin D.** Vitamin D is connected to testosterone production. Sources: sunlight or foods like fatty fish, egg yolks, and fortified foods like milk and cereal.

Recipes: Egg Muffin Cup with Bacon, Cottage Pie, Roast Chicken with Root Vegetables.

Building a strong foundation for your body's growth and development is a process that requires time and patience. Each phase must be built with integrity to withstand wear and tear and remain strong throughout the years. While the changes your body is going through can be uncomfortable, in chapter 2 we will take a deeper look at how nutrition can be a tool in managing these changes. We will examine the macronutrients, micronutrients, and hydration protocols that can support your bone health and muscle development, balance hormones, boost brain and cognitive development, and optimize performance and recovery.

CHAPTER TWO

OPTIMIZING NUTRITION FOR PERFORMANCE AND RECOVERY

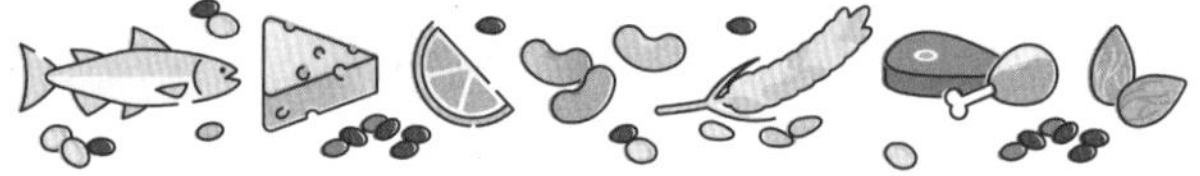

Nutrition is also a valuable component that can help athletes both protect themselves and improve performance.

—Bill Toomey

In chapter 1, we explored the changes that occur in your body during adolescence. We discussed how nutrition is a powerful tool in controlling your hormones, which in turn affect bone health, muscle development, and brain and cognitive function. In this chapter, we will take a deeper look into the macronutrients, micronutrients, and hydration protocols that create an optimal nutrition environment that sets you up for improving performance and recovery.

Just as you would carefully select the best materials and tools to construct a custom home that can withstand environmental pressures, in this chapter, we will help you set up your body to grow, develop, and endure the demands of running, school, and other life activities. These essential tools are the nutrients you use to fuel: macronutrients, micronutrients, and hydration. But before we take a closer look, let's first understand two key concepts: metabolism and energy availability.

Have you ever been running along and reached a point in the run where your legs start to feel heavy, your breathing is labored, and you feel like you're running through quicksand? You may have heard the term hitting the wall; that is what it feels like—when your energy reserves are so depleted that you can't imagine running another step.

Think of your metabolism as the engine that keeps your body running. Just like your home's furnace, it needs fuel to operate. If it's not getting enough power, it won't be able to keep up with your physical activity, leading to that feeling of hitting the wall.

Your metabolic rate—the speed at which your body burns fuel—varies from person to person. It is influenced by age, gender, body composition (the ratio of fat, muscle, and bone), activity level, and genetics. Hormonal changes or shifts in body composition can also impact how efficiently your metabolism performs.

Repeated instances of feeling like you've hit the wall can lead to low energy availability (LEA). This condition can affect metabolism, cause hormonal imbalance and fatigue, and impair immune function, thereby increasing the risk of injury and illness. For more detailed information, refer to page 85 in chapter 4.

MACRONUTRIENTS

Macronutrients are the nutrients consumed in significant amounts throughout the day to keep your body functioning normally. Just as the material, size, and placement of the building blocks you chose for your house impact its structural integrity, framing, and protection, macronutrients are the building blocks of your body. The quality, amounts, and timing of when you consume them all affect the functions they support, such as providing the energy you need for daily activities, running, and mental tasks; helping build muscle; repairing damaged tissue; regulating your body temperature; and protecting your organs. Macronutrients, which include carbohydrates, proteins, and fats, are the key to your body's performance.[18]

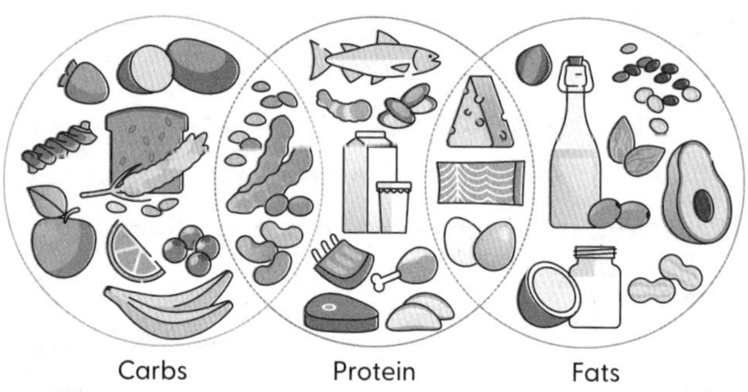

CARBOHYDRATES

Carbohydrates, often referred to as the fuel for your body, are the primary source of energy. Think of them as the power that

18 Laura K. Purcell, "Sport Nutrition for Young Athletes," *Paediatrics & Child Health* 18, no. 4 (April 18, 2013): 200–205, https://doi.org/10.1093/pch/18.4.200.

drives the construction equipment needed to build your house. When you consume carbohydrate-rich foods like grains and vegetables, your body breaks them down into glucose, a form of sugar that fuels the cells powering your muscles. This energy is what keeps you going during your workouts and daily activities.

Studies have shown that adolescents store less glycogen than adults; therefore, carbohydrates should make up the majority of the increased caloric needs of the adolescent athlete.[19] Regardless of age, low carbohydrate intake in athletes can cause poor energy levels if glycogen stores become too depleted, causing you to feel sluggish in your workouts and to have difficulty concentrating in the classroom.

All carbohydrates are not created equal. There are complex carbohydrates and simple carbohydrates.

COMPLEX CARBOHYDRATES

Complex carbohydrates, the essential building blocks for your body's energy needs, are made of long chains of sugar molecules that take longer for your body to break down and digest. This slow digestion is a good thing! It allows for a gradual release of glucose into your bloodstream, providing a steady energy source over an extended period. The sustained release of energy from complex carbohydrates ensures that you have a consistent and constant supply of power, which helps delay the onset of fatigue and stabilize blood sugar, preventing the feeling of energy highs and crashes.[20]

---

19 JohnEric W. Smith, Megan E. Holmes, and Matthew J. McAllister, "Nutritional Considerations for Performance in Young Athletes," *Journal of Sports Medicine* 2015 (2015): 1–13.

20 Smith, Holmes, and McAllister, "Nutritional Considerations for Performance in Young Athletes."

Complex carbohydrates also contain dietary fiber, which is essential for your intake as it promotes a healthy digestive system for regular bowel movements. High-fiber foods like fruits and vegetables also contain water, which can improve your overall hydration. Fiber also acts as a prebiotic, feeding beneficial bacteria into your gut. A healthy gut microbiome is associated with better digestion, nutrient absorption, and immune function.[21]

WHAT IS A GUT MICROBIOME?

The community of bacteria in your stomach helps keep your immune system strong, aids in digestion, and even affects your mood and energy levels. You can support a healthy gut microbiome by eating a lot of fruits, vegetables, whole grains, and prebiotic foods like yogurt and kefir. See the Homemade Granola and Yogurt Bowl recipe on page 215.

Note: As a runner, you need to be aware of the timing of consuming dietary fiber. Learn more about when to avoid high-fiber meals in chapter 3.

SIMPLE CARBOHYDRATES

Whereas complex carbohydrates are made of long chains of sugar molecules, simple carbohydrates are made of just a few sugar molecules. Unlike the building blocks of complex carbohydrates, they are easy to break down and digest, making them immediately available for your muscles to access and ideal for

21 Alex E. Mohr et al., "The Athletic Gut Microbiota," *Journal of the International Society of Sports Nutrition* 17, no. 1 (May 12, 2020), https://doi.org/10.1186/s12970-020-00353-w.

snacks before, during, and after workouts. You will learn more about this in chapter 3. Because they spike your blood sugar, they should be used in moderation, as too much at the wrong time can leave you feeling fatigued.

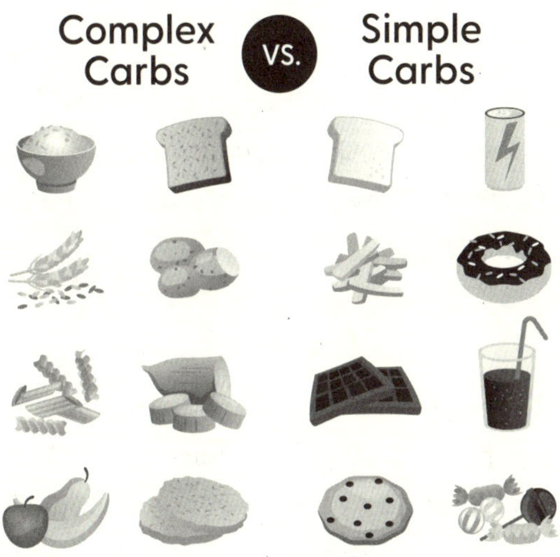

To better understand how much carbohydrate you may need to fuel your body and properly enhance your running and training, the Youth Running Consensus Statement recommends 6 to 10g carbohydrate/kg/day.[22] You might be more familiar with thinking of food intake in terms of calories, so the equivalent in calories is also shown on the next page. See table A.1 (page 248) for how to convert pounds to kilograms, and see table A.2 (page 249) for how to convert grams of carbohydrate to calories.

22 Brian J. Krabak et al., "Youth Running Consensus Statement: Minimising Risk of Injury and Illness in Youth Runners," *British Journal of Sports Medicine* 55, no. 6 (October 29, 2020): 305–18, https://doi.org/10.1136/bjsports-2020-102518.

Average carbohydrate intake for a young female runner who weighs 56 kilograms:

336 to 560g/day or 1344 to 2240 calories/day

Average carbohydrate intake for a young male runner who weighs 61 kilograms:

366 to 610g/day or 1464 to 2440 calories/day

To apply these calculations to yourself and determine your specific needs, see "How to Create Your Personal Nutrition Profile" on page 251.

PROTEIN

While carbohydrates are the primary fuel source for your body's energy supply, protein plays a crucial role in maintaining a sound structure. Proteins are the architects of muscle building and the engineers of tissue repair, ensuring your body is always ready for daily activities and running.

Amino acids, the building blocks of proteins, are small molecules that bind together to form these vital nutrients. There are 9 essential amino acids and 11 non-essential amino acids. However, our bodies cannot produce essential amino acids, so we must obtain them from food.

Animal Protein Sources:

- Meat: beef, poultry, pork
- Fish: salmon, tuna, cod
- Eggs
- Dairy products: milk, cheese, yogurt

Plant-Based Protein Sources:

- Quinoa
- Buckwheat
- Soy products: beans, tofu, tempeh, edamame
- Chia seeds, which also provide omega-3 fatty acids
- Hemp seeds: a powerhouse that are a source of all essential amino acids, healthy fats, and fiber.
- Spirulina is a high-protein and nutrient-dense blue-green algae. It is a great option for adding to smoothies (see page 204).

To better understand how much protein you need to help your body repair and rebuild, the Youth Running Consensus Statement recommends 1.2 to 2.0 g/kg/day.[23] As with the carbohydrates, see table A.2 on page 249 for how to convert grams of protein to calories.

Average protein intake for the young female runner who weighs 56 kilograms:

67 to 112g/day or 268 to 448 calories/day

Average protein intake for a young male runner who weighs 61 kilograms:

73 to 122g or 292 to 488 calories/day

You can also use these guidelines to determine your specific needs. See "How to Create Your Personal Nutrition Profile" on page 251.

Protein should primarily come from whole food sources, spaced in 20- to 30-gram servings throughout the day. To prevent muscle breakdown, focus on consuming lean protein with each meal and snack throughout the day, most specifically 20 grams of protein following a workout. You can read more about protein timing in chapter 3.

Examples of 20g Protein:

→ 3 eggs

→ 3 to 4 ounces chicken, pork, beef, or fish

→ 8 to 9 ounces tofu

→ 20 ounces milk

→ 1 cup Greek yogurt

---

23 Krabak et al., "Youth Running Consensus Statement."

- → ¾ cup cottage cheese
- → ½ cup legumes[24]

FAT

Carbohydrates are the primary fuel of our body's energy supply. Proteins offer structural integrity by coming in to repair and rebuild damaged muscle tissue. Fats are an added layer of protection and support, like insulation and reinforcement beams. Fats insulate the body, regulating temperature and protecting organs. They are needed to absorb fat-soluble vitamins (A, D, E, and K) and to produce cholesterol and sex hormones.

Fats are a dense energy source providing more than twice the calories per gram compared to carbohydrates and protein. During high-intensity exercise, simple carbohydrates are used first for quick energy but are quickly depleted. As exercise lasts longer or intensity decreases, the body gradually shifts to using fats, which are metabolized more slowly and provide sustained energy.

The science shows that adolescents can more easily use fat stores as a fuel source than adults. Fat should constitute 20 to 35 percent of your daily intake, with the majority coming from heart-healthy unsaturated fats.[25]

To better understand the amount of healthy fats you need to consume for energy, absorbing vitamins, and hormone

---

24 Erin K. Berg, "Performance Nutrition for the Adolescent Athlete," *Clinical Journal of Sport Medicine 29*, no. 5 (September 2019): 345–52, https://doi.org/10.1097/jsm.0000000000000744.

25 Krabak et al., "Youth Running Consensus Statement."

production, the Youth Running Consensus Statement recommends 1 to 2.0g/kg/day.[26] As with the carbohydrates and protein, see table A.2 in the Appendix for how to convert grams of fat to calories.

Average fat intake for a young female runner who weighs 56 kilograms:

56 to 112g/day or 504 to 1008 calories/day

Average fat intake for a young male runner who weighs 61 kilograms:

61 to 122g or 549 to 1098 calories/day

Remember, you can apply these, and other, calculations to yourself and determine your specific needs by following the steps in "Creating Your Personal Nutrition Profile," in the Appendix.

Healthy Nutrition Fats

26 Krabak et al., "Youth Running Consensus Statement."

EXAMPLES OF HEALTHY FAT

- → Fish
- → Avocado
- → Nuts, seeds, and olive oil
- → Eggs
- → Beans
- → Omega-3 fortified breads and cereals

MICRONUTRIENTS

Whereas macronutrients are the building blocks, micronutrients are the tools needed to fine-tune the construction. These include vitamins and minerals vital to energy production, immune function, and bone and muscle health. The three essential micronutrients for the young runner are iron, calcium, and vitamin D.[27] They are consumed in small amounts and typically measured in milligrams. Below you'll find information for recommended daily allowances of these three micronutrients for females and males between the ages of 10 and 24. I'm using this age range because the World Health Organization (WHO) defines adolescence as the ages of 10 to 19 years and youth as between 15 and 24 years, while young people encompass the entire age group of 10- to 24-year-olds.[28]

27 Christian Hecht et al., "Nutritional Recommendations for the Young Athlete: Current Concept Review," Journal of the Pediatric Orthopaedic Society of North America 5, no. 1 (February 1, 2023), https://doi.org/10.55275/JPOSNA-2023-599.

28 Purcell, "Sport Nutrition for Young Athletes."

IRON

Iron is an essential mineral that fuels the bodily functions that directly affect your running: oxygen transport, energy production, and immune system function. Iron carries oxygen to your muscles and organs, ensuring they receive the oxygen supply for optimal performance. Insufficient iron intake may result in fatigue and weakness, shortness of breath (especially during physical exercise), dizziness or lightheadedness, cold hands and feet, pica (characterized by cravings for non-food items like ice, dirt, etc.), and restless leg syndrome (RLS), which results in an urge to move your legs and can cause the sensation of crawling, itching, or a deep ache in your legs.

The recommended daily allowance (RDA)—the average daily intake sufficient to meet the nutrient requirements of nearly all healthy individuals in a particular life stage and gender group—for children ages 10 to 13 is about 8mg of iron daily. This increases to 15mg for females ages 14 to 18 and 11mg for males ages 14 to 18. Iron needs continue to increase for girls ages 19 to 24, to 18mg/day, and lowers back down for boys to 8mg/day.[29]

IRON SOURCES

Iron is an important micronutrient for youth athletes and comes in two forms: heme iron and non-heme iron. Heme iron, found in meat, fish, and poultry, is easily absorbed by the body. Non-heme iron, found in eggs and plant-based foods like beans, lentils, tofu, nuts and seeds, whole grains, and vegetables, is less readily absorbed. However, you can enhance its absorption

29 Jai K. Das et al., "Nutrition in Adolescents: Physiology, Metabolism, and Nutritional Needs," *Annals of the New York Academy of Sciences* 1393, no. 1 (April 24, 2017): 21–33, https://doi.org/10.1111/nyas.13330.

by pairing iron-rich foods with foods high in vitamin C, like bell peppers; broccoli and Brussels sprouts; strawberries; and oranges.[30]

Iron-rich recipes in chapter 7: Thai Green Curry with Chicken and Sweet Potatoes, Sardine Toast, and White Bean, Potato, and Broccoli Soup.

CALCIUM

Calcium is the most abundant mineral in the body. It is primarily used in the growth of bone mineral density and the immune system, which was presented in chapter 1. Calcium is the building block of your bones and, as you learned in chapter 1, you gain 90 percent of your adult bone mass in your adolescent years. There are currently no specific guidelines of calcium intake for youth athletes, so we are following the RDA of the National Institutes of Health.

The National Institutes of Health RDA for children ages 10 to 18 is to consume about 1300mg of calcium daily, while young adults ages 19 to 24 should consume 1000mg/day.[31]

Dairy and fortified soy alternatives like yogurt and milk are excellent sources of calcium. Vegetables like cooked spinach, bok choy, and kale are also excellent sources. Tofu and tahini are great plant-based proteins that are also high in calcium. Canned salmon and fortified fruit juices like grapefruit and orange juice are also good sources. Including these foods in your diet can help you meet your daily calcium needs.

---

30 National Institutes of Health, "Office of Dietary Supplements–Iron," Nih.gov, August 17, 2023, https://ods.od.nih.gov/factsheets/Iron-Consumer.

31 "Dietary Guidelines for Americans," Dietaryguidelines.gov, 2020, https://www.dietaryguidelines.gov.

Calcium-rich recipes in chapter 7: Blueberry Peach Yogurt Smoothie, Caesar Salad with Toasted Walnuts, and Tofu Buddha Bowl.

VITAMIN D

Vitamin D is essential to bone health and our immune and muscular systems. Studies show that 80 percent of young athletes who train and compete indoors or during the winter are deficient in vitamin D, compared to 48 percent of their outdoor peers. Female athletes are at higher risk for vitamin D deficiency. Low iron levels increase the risk of vitamin D deficiency in young athletes.

Scientific studies on vitamin D in the adolescent population are inconclusive. However, factors that put you at risk for vitamin D deficiency are:

- → Limited sun exposure, such as spending extended periods of training indoors
- → Having dark skin. Pigment in persons with darker skin blocks sunlight absorption, an essential process for vitamin D production
- → Wearing protective clothing

Vitamin D deficiency has been linked to muscle function, muscle pain and weakness, and inflammation.[32] The National Institutes of Health RDA for children and young adults ages 10 to 24 is 15mcg (600IU) of vitamin D daily.[33]

32 Das et al., "Nutrition in Adolescents"

33 Desbrow, "Youth Athlete Development and Nutrition."

Excellent food sources of vitamin D include:

- → Salmon, tuna, tilapia, and flounder
- → Dairy and fortified soy alternatives like milk and yogurt
- → Mushrooms
- → Orange juice
- → Plant-based milks like unsweetened almond milk and rice beverages

Vitamin D–rich recipes in chapter 7: Fish Burrito with Creole Seasoning, Tuna Salad with Green Goddess Dressing, and Cottage Pie.

MICRONUTRIENT DEFICIENCY

What should I do if I think I'm deficient in a micronutrient? If you have micronutrient deficiency symptoms, it is best to consult a healthcare professional, such as your doctor or a registered sports dietitian, to discuss your concerns. They can help assess your symptoms and determine if further testing is considered. They may recommend blood tests to confirm the deficiency and identify the underlying cause. Consider taking note of your symptoms so that you can easily explain what you're experiencing when you see them. Once you make any doctor-recommended changes to your nutrition, keep a journal to track your progress.

HYDRATION

Proper hydration is not just a necessity; it's one of the most powerful tools in your toolbox. It's the key to transporting nutrients from food throughout your body, ensuring your organs and systems function optimally. Think of it like a well-functioning plumbing system in your house, efficiently distributing water. But it's not just about the internal systems. Hydration also plays a crucial role in your physical performance. It can be the difference between a sluggish, fatigued run and a powerful, energized one. It regulates your body temperature, removes waste, and lubricates tissues. These lubricated tissues are your secret weapon in maintaining joint health, flexibility, mobility, and protection against injury. So, hydration is not just about quenching your thirst; it's about enhancing your performance and protecting your body.

Electrolytes are minerals that carry an electrical charge when dissolved in water, and they are essential in maintaining hydration and regulating muscle function. By replenishing these electrolytes, you can effectively prevent dehydration, maintain optimal performance, and reduce the risk of heat-related illnesses.

Benefits of Drinking Water

When you exercise in hot conditions, your body must stay cool to avoid overheating. Adults primarily rely on sweating to cool down, whereas in adolescents other physiological processes, like redistributing blood flow on the skin's surface, release heat. For this to happen effectively, you must drink enough fluids to stay hydrated and comfortable while running.

Dehydration is a serious matter, especially when it comes to exercise. If you're sweating and not replenishing fluids as recommended, this can lead to significant health risks. Research has shown that even a 2 percent loss of your total body weight due to dehydration can significantly impair your performance.[34] To put it into perspective, if you weigh 130 pounds and find yourself weighing 127.4 pounds after exercise, that's a 2 percent loss, indicating dehydration. This can lead to decreased blood volume, making it harder for your heart to pump blood to the muscles you're using to run. So, it's not something to take lightly. It can directly impact your performance and overall health.

Recognizing the signs of dehydration is the first step in maintaining your well-being and performance. These signs may include decreased energy, feeling faint or dizzy, and irritability. If you experience these signs, taking a break from your workout is a good idea—sip on some water with electrolytes, and consume a snack of simple carbohydrates. This straightforward approach will help replenish your body and get you back on track. Immediate action is key to preventing further dehydration and its negative effects.

---

34 Michael N. Sawka et al., "American College of Sports Medicine Position Stand. Exercise and Fluid Replacement," *Medicine and Science in Sports and Exercise*, February 1, 2007, https://pubmed.ncbi.nlm.nih.gov/17277604.

Another reliable indicator of dehydration is the color of your urine:

COLOR	HYDRATION LEVEL
Light Yellow	Hydrated
Yellow	Good
Dark Yellow	Likely Dehydrated
Light Orange	Dehydrated

OVERHYDRATION

Sodium is an important electrolyte that regulates fluid balance in your body. It is just as important to understand the risks of overhydration that can occur when you drink too much water and the sodium levels in your blood become too diluted. This is called hyponatremia. Signs of overhydration may include headache, confusion, muscle weakness, nausea or vomiting, or even loss of consciousness. If you experience these symptoms or are witnessing a teammate experience these symptoms, it is important to seek medical attention immediately.[35]

Here is a breakdown of how electrolytes work together.

ELECTROLYTE	FUNCTION
Sodium	Sodium helps balance your body's water levels, essential for staying hydrated during running. It also plays a significant role in muscle contraction, allowing your muscles to move efficiently when you run.

35 Douglas J. Casa et al., "Fluid Needs for Training, Competition, and Recovery in Track-and-Field Athletes," *International Journal of Sport Nutrition and Exercise Metabolism* 29, no. 2 (2019): 175–80, https://doi.org/10.1123/ijsnem.2018-0374.

Potassium	Potassium fuels your muscles and nerves, ensuring your muscles are working correctly and the nerve signals are firing to help you maintain coordination and agility.
Calcium	You learned about the role of calcium in building strong bones and muscles to support you while you're running low on micronutrients. Adding electrolytes to your water is another way to ensure you are meeting your daily calcium requirements.
Magnesium	Magnesium's benefits are twofold: it not only provides energy to your muscles for running but also helps them relax, aiding in recovery after your workout.
Chloride	Chloride is the electrolyte that works behind the scenes and helps you absorb other nutrients to fuel your running.

Read more about fluid timing and how to create your hydration profile in the Appendix (see table A.3 on page 250).

SUPPLEMENTATION

You hear about supplements in your social media feeds, from peers, and maybe even from coaches and parents. Current studies show that youth athletes' most frequently used supplements are vitamins and minerals, and protein powders. Females more regularly use supplements associated with health, recovery, and replacing an inadequate diet. Males are more likely to report taking supplements for enhanced performance.36

The marketing messages can be strong and convincing; most sell a message of overall health and well-being, better performance, and faster recovery. Supplements are a multibillion-dollar business, growing as many athletes seek that magic bullet or a shortcut. They come in the form of drinks, powders,

36 McDowall, "Supplement Use by Young Athletes."

or pills, and you may be consuming one or more without a second thought. There are a few key things to understand about supplements:

→ Understand the role of the US Food and Drug Administration (FDA) in supplement regulation. Unlike drugs, the FDA only checks the safety and efficacy of supplements after they're available to the consumer. This means it's your responsibility to research and evaluate the safety and effectiveness of supplements before using them, empowering you to make informed decisions about your health.[37]

→ Due to ethical concerns, there is a lack of research on supplementation in adolescents. This means that the potential long-term risks of supplement use remain unknown. This underscores the need for caution and awareness, encouraging youth athletes to consider the potential risks before using supplements.[38]

→ Most experts, including the information in this book, advocate a food-first approach to nutrition. This means most of your nutrients should come from whole, minimally processed foods like fruits, vegetables, whole grains, lean proteins, and healthy fats. These foods are rich in essential vitamins, minerals, and fiber. A food-first approach also ensures you get a diverse range of nutrients to support your overall well-being.

---

37 McDowall, "Supplement Use by Young Athletes."

38 Smith, Holmes, and McAllister, "Nutritional Considerations for Performance in Young Athletes."

→ Youth athletes are only advised to use dietary supplements if a doctor or a registered sports dietitian determines a clinical need. Supplements should only be used when a specific health condition or deficiency cannot be adequately addressed through a balanced diet. This underscores the importance of seeking professional guidance before considering supplement use.[39]

Knowledge is power, so let's ensure you understand some of the most used supplements, how and why they are used, their risks, and how to research them—remembering that supplements cannot replace real food.

MULTIVITAMINS

Multivitamins contain a combination of vitamins and minerals meant to supplement a deficiency in one's energy intake. According to the federal government's Dietary Guidelines, Americans should get most of their nutrients from food and beverages. Foods contain vitamins, minerals, dietary fiber, and other health components. Common deficiencies in the diet of adolescent athletes are calcium, vitamin D, and iron.[40] Read the "Micronutrients" section on page 35 for natural food sources of these vitamins and minerals.

PROTEIN POWDERS

As discussed in the "Macronutrients" section on page 26, protein is essential to the diet for muscle repair and immune function. Protein in the form of a supplement is extracted from animal or plant-based sources, which range from cow's

39 Hecht et al., "Nutritional Recommendations for the Young Athlete."

40 Purcell, "Sport Nutrition for Young Athletes."

milk and eggs to peas, rice, and soy. Naturally occurring carbohydrates, fats, minerals, and fiber are often removed during processing, while supplementary nutrients, herbs, and sweeteners may be added.

See the "Protein" section on page 30 for recommended protein intake and accurate food protein sources. If you are a vegetarian or vegan and your doctor or sports dietitian has determined that you could benefit from supplementing with a protein powder, here are two protein powders to note.

Whey Protein Powder

Whey protein is the protein from whey, the watery portion of milk that separates from the curds when making cheese. Whey is processed to reduce fat and lactose content, leaving mainly protein. Whey protein isolate may be better for people with lactose intolerance, but it's not for people with milk allergies.

Studies show that whey protein is highly bioavailable, quickly digested and absorbed by the body, making it ideal for muscle recovery. It also contains all nine essential amino acids, which are the building blocks of protein and necessary for muscle growth and repair.[41]

Pea Protein Powder

Pea protein powder is a plant-based protein supplement extracted from yellow peas. It is a popular option for people looking for a vegan or allergen-friendly protein source, as it is free from dairy, soy, and gluten.

41 Ralf Jäger, "International Society of Sports Nutrition Position Stand: Protein and Exercise," *Journal of the International Society of Sports Nutrition* 14, no. 1 (June 20, 2017), https://doi.org/10.1186/s12970-017-0177-8.

CREATINE

Creatine is a compound naturally derived from three essential amino acids—arginine, glycine, and methionine. It is naturally produced in the kidneys, liver, and pancreas, and our bodies produce about 1g/day. Supplementation with creatine has been shown to improve strength, power, and muscle mass in adolescent athletes. However, it is not recommended for adolescents under 18 due to limited research on its long-term safety in this population.[42] Real food sources: red meat, poultry, fish, pork, dairy products, whole grains, legumes, nuts and seeds, and vegetables.

OTHER PERFORMANCE BOOSTERS

While protein powders and other supplements may help fill the gaps in nutrition deficiencies, performance-enhancing substances, such as stimulants, should be used with care.

Caffeine

Caffeine is a natural stimulant compound found in various plants, most notably in coffee beans, tea leaves, cacao pods (used to make chocolate), and kola nuts. Caffeine has been proven to improve focus and energy levels, reduce fatigue, and improve endurance.[43] However, there is also evidence that caffeine can have adverse side effects such as anxiety, insomnia, and irregular heartbeat. Adolescent athletes should use caffeine in moderation and have an awareness of your tolerance and sensitivity to caffeine.

---

42 McDowall, "Supplement Use by Young Athletes."

43 Jorge Lorenzo Calvo et al., "Caffeine and Cognitive Functions in Sports: A Systematic Review and Meta-Analysis," *Nutrients* 13, no. 3 (March 6, 2021), https://doi.org/10.3390/nu13030868.

Energy Drinks

I get it; you are looking for a way to beat the afternoon slump before practice, or you're drinking an energy drink that a teammate handed you. Caffeine is a natural stimulant and, if used moderately, is an effective ergogenic aid; however, some energy drinks have close to 200mg of caffeine and are also blended with sugar, vitamins, amino acids, and herbal extracts. Excessive consumption of energy drinks can lead to adverse health effects, including increased heart rate, insomnia, anxiety, dehydration, and potential interactions with medications or other substances.[44]

Think of the cycle the stimulants put you in. You have an energy drink at 5 p.m. At 10 p.m., that caffeine still pumps through your body, making it difficult to wind down and sleep. You're up a few hours past bedtime but must wake up at 7 a.m. for your school day. You go into the day already tired, and over time, the fatigue builds, and you're requiring an energy drink every afternoon to get through practice. And the cycle perpetuates.

You can naturally combat the afternoon energy slump by managing blood sugar levels with adequate fueling and hydrating throughout the day. You will learn more about this in chapter 3.

HOW DO I RESEARCH A SUPPLEMENT?

If you choose to take a supplement, you want to ensure that the product is tested and certified safe by a third-party

44 National Center for Complementary and Integrative Health, "Energy Drinks," NCCIH, July 2018, https://www.nccih.nih.gov/health/energy-drinks; Sale and Elliott-Sale, "Nutrition and Athlete Bone Health."

company like the National Safety Foundation (NSF), www.nsfcertifiedsport.com or Informed-Sport, www.informedsport.com. Third-party testing means that an organization or experts in the product being tested are independent of the product and have no vested interest in the outcome of the test. NSF has developed certification guidelines to prevent tampering, to verify label claims against the contents, and to ensure they don't contain banned substances.

QUESTIONS TO CONSIDER BEFORE BUYING A SUPPLEMENT

Is it safe? The supplement should be NSF-certified and free of banned substances.

Is it effective? There should be scientific evidence to support the effectiveness.

Do I need it? A doctor should determine your clinical need for the supplement that nutrition cannot meet. Work with a Registered Sports Dietitian to fine-tune your nutrition and assist in selecting any supplements.

Will I use it? The supplement should quickly adapt to your already busy lifestyle.

To review, supplements are not a replacement for getting your nutrients from whole, minimally processed foods. If you believe that you might be deficient in a vitamin or mineral or need aid in recovering faster, consult with your doctor or a registered sports dietitian so that the proper blood work can be ordered to test for any deficiencies. To continue to explore, keep a food journal to track what nutrients you are taking in. A dietitian will find this helpful in seeing if any deficiencies can be met with food before supplementing.

In this chapter we learned that consuming enough food is necessary to your metabolism running efficiently. The nutrition tools we need in our toolbox are macronutrients: carbohydrates that provide energy, protein that builds and repairs muscles, and fats that protect organs and help produce hormones; and micronutrients that include vitamins and minerals and most specifically the key micronutrients for young runners: iron, calcium, and vitamin D. Hydration is one of our most powerful tools and is necessary for maintaining performance and preventing heat-related illnesses and injuries. And finally, we educated ourselves on supplements, learning that they should be used cautiously and only under the guidance of a medical professional. In chapter 3, we will start looking at how the timing of the use of these tools is important to make sure there is a steady supply of energy throughout the day and around your workouts.

CHAPTER THREE

STRATEGIC FUELING AND HYDRATION

First we eat, then we do everything else.

—M.F.K. Fisher

By taking the time to understand your physiology during this stage of life and the roles of macronutrients, micronutrients, and hydration in supporting your growth and development and optimizing your performance and recovery, you have built a strong foundation and framework for your house, constructed it with the best materials, and applied the finishing touches. Now, how do you keep your home running smoothly? You have school, workouts, races, and friends and family you want to spend time with. Just as one would manage the schedule of a home, you can strategically plan your nutrition and provide your body with the nutrients it needs to keep your mind sharp in the classroom, perform in your workouts and races, and recover quickly.

UNLOCKING THE POWER OF NUTRITION AND HYDRATION TIMING

The goal of nutrition and hydration timing is to provide a steady release of energy with the macronutrients your body can best utilize at different times of the day and around your workouts. Think of each meal as a building block. Your breakfast of complex carbohydrates, lean protein, and healthy fats establishes a strong base for the day, leveling up your liver and glycogen stores that were depleted overnight. If you don't do this, you begin your day depleted, creating a cascading effect that makes it difficult to fully restore after using energy in the classroom, which ultimately does not allow you to be at your best for afternoon practice. Your mid-morning snack builds off breakfast, a balanced lunch prepares you for afternoon practice, and simple carbohydrates before, during, and after your workout give you the quick release of energy to use during the workout and begin to immediately restore glycogen stores after. A balanced dinner helps your muscles repair and recover and sets you up for a good night's sleep so that you're ready to go again the next day. Maintaining hydration throughout the day is essential in transporting nutrients from the food you eat throughout the body and ensuring organs and systems are functioning optimally. Let's take a closer look at the nutrition that surrounds your workouts.

PRE-WORKOUT NUTRITION

The pre-workout meal or snack is a personalized strategy that ensures your liver and muscle glycogen stores are replenished to an optimal level. This approach recognizes that we all have different metabolism rates (page 25), and understanding your metabolism is crucial in finding what works best for you. For instance, some athletes I coach can consume a peanut butter and jelly sandwich within an hour of their workout, while others find this too heavy. Just like you practice race strategy, baton handoffs, and workouts specific to your event, you want to practice your fueling and hydration. By "practice," I mean experimenting with different foods, timings, and quantities to see what gives you the best energy and performance during your workouts. The best time to practice is every day and months before your big competitions.

It's common to have concerns about pre-workout nutrition: "I'm not hungry in the morning; if I eat, I have to stop to go to the bathroom; if I eat, I feel sick." These are valid concerns, and I want to encourage you that you have the power to find the right food and timing for your metabolism with patience and consistent practice. Studies show that repetitive exposure to nutrition before and during exercise can help train your gut to tolerate fuel intake and reduce exercise-associated gastrointestinal symptoms.[45] The suggested foods and timelines below are a starting point. By taking notes on what you eat and how you feel, you can empower yourself to understand and respond to your body's needs.

If you haven't been eating anything before your runs, start small, and then, over time, you can work up to taking in more

45 Isabel G. Martinez et al., "The Effect of Gut-Training and Feeding-Challenge on Markers of Gastrointestinal Status in Response to Endurance Exercise: A Systematic Literature Review," *Sports Medicine*, April 15, 2023, https://doi.org/10.1007/s40279-023-01841-0.

nutrition as your body adapts. Ideas for starting small: 4 ounces of juice, a banana, half of a plain bagel, or low-fiber cereal, like Cheerios. You can gradually add more fuel as your body adapts, like the Peanut Butter and Jam Overnight Oats (page 220) or the Maple Banana Custard Oatmeal (page 142).

The timing of your workout and the time elapsed since your last meal are fundamental in planning your pre-workout nutrition. Think of your body's glycogen stores as the energy source for your workout and topping them off as adding a fresh coat of paint to your house. If you recently had a balanced meal and allowed time for digestion, this is a strong base. Your body already has a supply of energy.

If you're on your way to a workout and it's been a few hours since you ate, a banana or sports gels/chews are simple carbohydrates that act like instant energy, replenishing your glycogen stores for immediate use.

You also might consider a mini-meal or snack 90 minutes to two hours before your workout.

Mini-meal Examples:

- Homemade Granola and Yogurt Bowl (page 215)
- Whole-grain toast with peanut butter and banana slices

Snack Examples:

- No-Bake Energy Bar (page 211)
- Nuts and dried fruit

DURING-WORKOUT NUTRITION

Okay, you've shown up to practice and are ready to go. Just as a house requires ongoing maintenance to stay in good condition, your body needs continuous energy replenishment during long workouts. Regularly consuming simple carbohydrates during long workouts ensures that your body remains fueled, preventing energy depletion and keeping you performing at your best.

Like pre-run nutrition, the closer you are to the workout, the simpler the fuel needs to be. For workouts lasting more than 60 minutes, incorporating simple carbohydrates every 30 minutes will keep your energy stores topped off. An example would be consuming a sports gel or a few sports chews.

Proper fueling during your workout makes the post-workout repair process more efficient. This is akin to keeping a house in good condition so that any necessary repairs are less extensive. When you maintain energy levels during the workout, there's less damage to repair afterward, allowing your body to focus on strengthening muscles rather than trying to come back from severe depletion.

POST-WORKOUT NUTRITION

Just as the initial moments after identifying damage in a house are crucial for effective repairs, the first 30 minutes post-workout are a key time to kickstart your body's recovery. During this period, your body is most efficient at synthesizing glucose to rebuild energy stores and repair muscles.[46] Aim for a combination of carbohydrates and protein within 30 minutes post-workout.

---

46 Jennifer Sacheck and Nicole Schultz, "Optimal Nutrition for Youth Athletes: Food Sources and Fuel Timing," American College of Sports Medicine, acsm.org, 2017, https://www.acsm.org/docs/default-source/nyshsi_resources/resources/nyshsi-optimal-nutrition-for-youth-athletes.pdf.

By consuming carbohydrates immediately after your workout, your body quickly replenishes glycogen stores. Proteins are essential for muscle repair and growth. A balanced post-workout snack could be a smoothie with carbohydrates and protein, or chocolate milk and a No-Bake Energy Bar (page 211). Other options include a granola bar or pretzels paired with a sports drink.

After starting to replenish your glycogen stores right after your workout, you can then focus on having a balanced meal of complex carbohydrates, lean protein, and fats within two hours, for example: Sheet Pan Greek Turkey Meatballs and Vegetables with Lemony Rice (page 189).

DAYS LEADING UP TO THE RACE

In chapter 2 we discussed the importance of dietary fiber, which you are getting from the complex carbohydrates you're consuming, such as fruits and vegetables. The physiological demands of race day (travel, veering from your normal food intake, pre-race nerves) add another layer of stress and can result in unwanted GI distress. There are nutrition choices that you can make leading up to race day to prevent this from happening.

TIPS

→ Avoid fried foods

→ Avoid spicy foods

→ Replace brown rice with white rice

→ Replace whole wheat bread with white bread

WHAT DOES THIS LOOK LIKE IN DAY-TO-DAY LIFE?

Just like your home's schedule may change based on changes in routines, priorities, or unexpected events, your activity level, training schedule, and goals may change, so being able to take these basic principles and adjust them to your individual needs is important.

This is also a key area where coaches and parents can help by developing a protocol around what runners should bring to practice, holding organized hydration breaks, and providing post-workout hydration options. Read more about this in chapter 5: "Integrating Nutrition Education into Running Programs."

Here are a few sample timelines to get you started.

FUELING TIMELINE FOR AFTERNOON PRACTICE

TIME	TYPE OF FUEL	WHY	EXAMPLES
8:00 a.m. (Breakfast)	Complex carbohydrates, protein, fat	Tops off liver and glycogen stores and keeps you satisfied until your mid-morning snack.	Breakfast Burrito with Tots
11:00 a.m. (Mid-morning snack)	Snack with balanced macronutrients	Maintains blood glucose levels and keeps energy resources topped off until lunch.	Almond Butter Banana Bread with Chocolate Chips and Walnuts
1:00 p.m. (Lunch)	A balanced meal with protein and complex carbohydrates	Maintains blood glucose levels and keeps energy resources topped off for afternoon practice.	Tofu Poké Bowl with Spicy Mayo
3:30 p.m. (Pre-workout)	Simple carbohydrates	Pre-workout energy boost.	Banana, pretzels, Fig Newtons
4:00 p.m. (Workout)	Simple carbohydrates	Provides usable energy for the workout.	Sports gel or blocks
6:00 p.m. (Post-workout)	Simple carbohydrates with protein	Promotes recovery and begins the process of rebuilding energy stores and repairing muscles.	Chocolate milk, No-Bake Energy Bar (page 211)
7:00 p.m. (Dinner)	Balanced dinner with lean protein, carbohydrates, and fat	Provides balanced nutrition within two hours of practice to support recovery.	Roast Chicken with Root Vegetables
10:00 p.m. (Bedtime)	Anti-inflammatory and protein	Aids sleep and recovery by reducing inflammation and providing protein for muscle repair.	1 ounce of tart cherry juice concentrate in 8 ounces of water with Homemade Granola and Yogurt Bowl

RACE DAY

I have attended several track and field and cross-country events over the years. Often these events require meeting up at the school early in the day and being prepared to spend most of the day out on the course or the track, cheering on teammates, waiting for events, and trying to eat and time meals based on a schedule that may change. You also might have several hours before you're loading up on the bus to return home or back to your hotel, without access to a place where you can get the well-balanced recovery meal you need. The nutrition timing you practice in your day-to-day is just as important—if not more important—on race day, when you've pushed your body to its limit that day. So here are a few timelines to guide you as well as a blank timeline for you to create your own schedule.

FOR MIDDLE TO HIGH SCHOOL AGE RUNNERS

Encourage team contribution for foods brought to events. Coaches, parents, or teammates can coordinate bringing snack options for the team. An online tool like Signup Genius (www.signupgenius.com) can be used for signups to provide a well-rounded supply of snacks.

SAMPLE CHECKLIST

- → Extra water and electrolytes
- → Chocolate milk
- → Orange slices
- → Apple slices
- → Pretzels
- → Graham crackers
- → White bread with nut butter and jam
- → No-Bake Energy Bars (page 211)
- → Glorious Morning Muffins (page 213)
- → Almond Butter Banana Bread with Chocolate Chips and Walnuts (page 209)
- → The Ultimate Oatmeal Raisin Cookie (page 234)

FUELING TIMELINE FOR RACE DAY WITH ONE EVENT IN THE MORNING

TIME	TYPE OF FUEL	WHY	EXAMPLES
3 to 4 hours before your race time	Complex carbohydrates with protein and fat	Provides sustained energy and helps top off liver and glycogen stores for optimal performance during the race.	Waffle Breakfast Sandwich—a portable option if you need to eat it on the way to the race. If you are at an away event: eggs, lean protein, and a carbohydrate like breakfast potatoes from the hotel breakfast bar. If this is not an option, come prepared with hard boiled eggs and ingredients to make a peanut butter and jelly sandwich.
15 to 30 minutes pre-race	Simple carbohydrate pre-race if needed	Provides immediate energy for the upcoming race.	Banana, sports gel, chews
30 minutes post-race	Snack to maintain blood glucose levels and replenish energy resources for future workouts	Promotes recovery and begins the process of rebuilding energy stores and repairing muscles.	Chocolate milk, graham crackers, pretzels, No-Bake Energy Bar
Within 2 hours post-race and later	Balanced meal within 2 hours of the race, consisting of lean protein, carbohydrate, and fat	Supports muscle repair, replenishes glycogen stores, and provides essential nutrients.	Pea Pesto Pasta Salad, fruit, The Ultimate Oatmeal Raisin Cookie

FUELING TIMELINE FOR RACE DAY WITH ONE EVENT IN THE AFTERNOON

TIME	TYPE OF FUEL	WHY	EXAMPLES
Breakfast upon waking	Complex carbohydrates with protein and fat	Provides sustained energy and helps top off liver and glycogen stores for optimal performance during the race.	Waffle Breakfast Sandwich—a portable option if you need to eat it on the way to the race. If you are at an away event: eggs, lean protein, and a carbohydrate like breakfast potatoes from the hotel breakfast bar. If this is not an option, come prepared with hard boiled eggs and ingredients to make a peanut butter and jelly sandwich.
2 to 3 hours before your race	Simple carbohydrates that your body can easily digest	Provides quick energy without causing digestive discomfort.	Plain bagel with jam, plain white rice
15 to 30 minutes pre-race	Simple carbohydrate pre-race if needed	Provides immediate energy for the upcoming race.	Banana, sports gel or chews
30 minutes post-race	Snack to maintain blood glucose levels and replenish energy resources for future workouts	Promotes recovery and begins the process of rebuilding energy stores and repairing muscles.	Chocolate milk, graham crackers, pretzels, No-Bake Energy Bar
Within 2 hours post race & throughout the day	Balanced meal within 2 hours of the race, consisting of lean protein, carbohydrate, and fat	Supports muscle repair, replenishes glycogen stores, and provides essential nutrients.	Apple-Almond Chicken Salad, fruit, The Ultimate Oatmeal Raisin Cookie

FUELING TIMELINE FOR RACE DAY WITH TWO EVENTS

TIME	TYPE OF FUEL	WHY	EXAMPLES
If you have 3 to 4 hours before race time	Complex carbohydrates with protein and fat	Provides sustained energy and helps top off liver and glycogen stores for optimal performance during the race.	Waffle Breakfast Sandwich —a portable option if you need to eat it on the way to the race. If you are at an away event: eggs, lean protein, and a carbohydrate like breakfast potatoes from the hotel breakfast bar. If this is not an option, come prepared with hard boiled eggs and ingredients to make a peanut butter and jelly sandwich.
If you have 2 hours or less	Simple carbohydrates that your body can easily digest	Provides quick energy without causing digestive discomfort.	Plain bagel with jam, plain white rice
15 to 30 minutes pre-race	Simple carbohydrate pre-race if needed	Provides immediate energy for the upcoming race.	Banana, sports gel or chews
30 minutes post-race	Snack to maintain blood glucose levels and replenish energy resources for future workouts	Supports recovery and prepares the body for subsequent activities.	Chocolate milk, graham crackers, pretzels, No-Bake Energy Bar)
If you have 2 hours+ before 2nd race	Simple carbohydrates that your body can easily digest	Provides quick energy without causing digestive discomfort.	Plain bagel with jam, plain white rice

If you have less than 2 hours before the next event	Simple carbohydrates that your body can easily digest	Provides quick energy for the upcoming event.	Banana, sports gel or chews, Waffle Breakfast Sandwich, Fig Newtons
Within 2 hours post race and then throughout the day	A balanced meal within 2 hours of the race, consisting of lean protein, carbohydrate, and fat	Supports muscle repair, replenishes glycogen stores, and provides essential nutrients.	Apple-Almond Chicken Salad, fruit, graham crackers, pretzels, The Ultimate Oatmeal Raisin Cookie

HYDRATION

To review, proper hydration is essential in transporting nutrients from food throughout the body and ensuring organs and systems function optimally—much like a well-functioning plumbing system ensures water is distributed efficiently throughout a house. It regulates body temperature, removes waste, and lubricates tissues. Lubricated tissues are essential for maintaining joint health, flexibility, mobility, and protection against injury.

On the next page are strategies for hydrating around your workout or race as well. See table A.3 on page 250 to learn how to fine-tune your unique hydration needs through a sweat rate test.

HYDRATION TIMING THROUGHOUT THE DAY

Upon Waking. 8 ounces of water

Throughout the Morning. 8 ounces of water

Pre-Workout (2 to 3 hours before). 16 to 24 ounces of water

During Workout. 4 to 12 ounces of fluid* every 15 minutes

Post Workout. Drink enough fluid to replace sweat losses. In general this is 3 cups of water per pound lost.**

* For events lasting less than 1 hour, water is sufficient. For events lasting longer than 1 hour or taking place in a hot environment, drink a sports drink.

** Consuming a sports drink or salty snacks post workout can help with rehydration by stimulating thirst and fluid retention.[47]

47 Sawka et al., "American College of Sports Medicine Position Stand. Exercise and Fluid Replacement."

CREATE YOUR OWN PLAN

TIME	TYPE OF FUEL	NOTES
8:00 a.m. (Breakfast)	Waffle Breakfast Sandwich 8 ounces of water	Filling
11:00 a.m. (Snack)	Apples with peanut butter 8 ounces of water	Needed more of a snack—was really hungry by lunch
1:00 p.m. (Lunch)	Tofu Poké Bowl with Spicy Mayo 4 ounces of water	Wish I'd brought a cookie
3:30 p.m. (Pre-workout fuel)	Banana 4 ounces of water	Enough
4:00 p.m. (During workout fuel)	2 gels for 2-hour practice 16 ounces of water	Hard practice—was glad I had both gels. With the heat I should have had more to drink, plus an electrolyte.

6:00 p.m. (Post-workout recovery fuel)	Chocolate milk and Glorious Morning Muffin 8 ounces of water	Perfect to hold me over until dinner
7:00 p.m. (Dinner)	Sheet Pan Greek Turkey Meatballs and Vegetables with Lemony Rice 16 ounces of water	Was still hungry so I had some cheese and crackers
10:00 p.m. (Bedtime)	Fudgy Chocolate Chia Pudding 8 ounces of water	Yum

CHAPTER FOUR

NAVIGATING NUTRITIONAL CHALLENGES

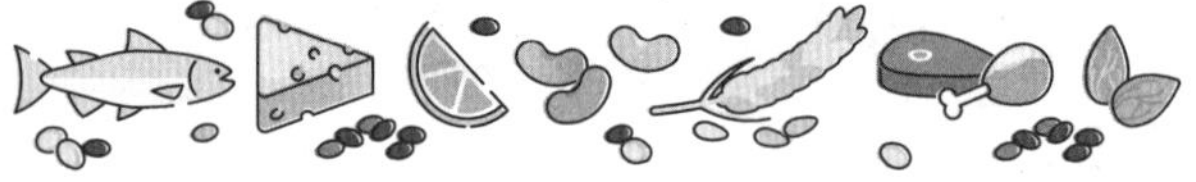

Let food be thy medicine and medicine be thy food.

—Hippocrates

One of the driving forces behind this book is my vision for a future where we don't see young runners in the news sharing their stories of disordered eating (DE), eating disorders (ED), the female and male athlete triads, or the inability to run due to low energy availability (LEA) that led to relative energy deficiency in sport (REDs); and additionally body image struggles. Instead, the headlines boldly highlight the shift in culture: that nutrition education is at the forefront of running programs, and other aspects of training like proper recovery and sleep are pillars of strong running programs. This knowledge empowers you, the athlete, your coaches, and your parents to make informed decisions about your nutrition, thereby fostering healthy running communities. Your voice can significantly impact our collective journey toward healthier running communities.

In the first three chapters, we focused on what is happening physiologically in your body during these formative years, how it relates to your running, and how you can optimize nutrition to support your performance and recovery. You've learned about the food-first approach, which emphasizes the importance of getting essential nutrients from whole foods rather than supplements. These nutrients include carbohydrates for energy, proteins for muscle repair, and fats for long-term energy. Just as a house needs a solid foundation to withstand wear and tear over time, your body requires a variety of nutrients to function optimally and sustain your running. This approach is fundamental to keeping your body strong, resilient, and capable of withstanding the demands of running and for preventing the nutritional challenges discussed in this chapter.

Nutritional challenges are multifaceted and may manifest in different ways throughout your running career. Therefore, it's not a singular opportunity for education but a continuous process of awareness. You may be worried that you are developing a disordered eating pattern, noticing habits of a teammate, or at different points, your energy intake may unintentionally not keep up with the increase in your workout load, leaving you tired, with restless sleep, and difficulty completing workouts. Once again, we will delve into these layers through the lens of your body as a custom-built house. Understanding the nuances of these nutrition challenges and how to seek support is crucial so that you can have self-awareness, help others who might be struggling, and continue to strengthen your foundation.

When discussing the various nutritional challenges you may encounter throughout your running career, it's important to understand how they are interconnected and how they may impact the structural integrity, not just of your bones and muscles, but all internal systems from your gut health to your mental health. In the case of ED and DE, the male and female athlete triads, and REDs, the athlete's nutrition intake is unbalanced. This may be intentional or unintentional. The unbalanced nutrition intake leads to low energy availability (LEA). Whether it's restrictive dieting (ED or DE) or not taking in enough energy to match an increase in exercise output, it puts stress on the frame of your body—each challenge has some common risks and symptoms, but some are stand-alone. Just like there are separate rooms in your home with different purposes, they are still under the same roof, with some shared health consequences.

Understanding the interconnectedness of these challenges can provide you with a comprehensive view that can empower you to make changes or seek the right help for your situation.

BODY IMAGE

Significant research has emerged over the past two decades concerning body image in children and adolescents, driven by concerns about the impact of poor body image on young people and its potential long-term effects, such as eating disorders. The research indicates that body dissatisfaction is prevalent among children, particularly girls, and increases with age, with boys becoming more concerned about muscularity during adolescence, and that social media significantly impacts how adolescents perceive their bodies, often contributing to body dissatisfaction.[48]

Body dissatisfaction occurs when a person persistently experiences negative thoughts and feelings about their body. It is an internal emotion and cognitive process that is influenced by external factors, such as pressure to meet a certain appearance ideal, like you need a stereotypical runner's body type to be a competitive runner. The dissatisfaction can lead to unhealthy behaviors, such as extreme dieting or over-exercising, increasing the risk of developing an eating disorder. [49]

WHAT ARE SIGNS THAT YOU MAY HAVE BODY IMAGE DISSATISFACTION?[50]

→ Repetitive dieting behaviors like frequent dieting, fasting, or skipping meals

→ Compulsive exercise patterns—for example, exercising in addition to your coach-assigned running workouts

→ Focusing on appearance—including hair, makeup, clothing, or striving for a certain body type

→ Negative self-talk and comparison—frequently comparing yourself to others and engaging in critical self-talk

---

48 Dian A. de Vries, Helen G. M. Vossen, and Paulien van der Kolk – van der Boom, "Social Media and Body Dissatisfaction: Investigating the Attenuating Role of Positive Parent–Adolescent Relationships," *Journal of Youth and Adolescence* 48, no. 3 (November 26, 2018): 527–36, https://doi.org/10.1007/s10964-018-0956-9.

49 Alyona Koulanova et al., "Ideas for Action: Exploring Strategies to Address Body Image Concerns for Adolescent Girls Involved in Sport," *Psychology of Sport and Exercise* 56 (September 2021): 102017, https://doi.org/10.1016/j.psychsport.2021.102017.

50 Melissa Rizk et al., "Physical Activity in Eating Disorders: A Systematic Review," *Nutrients* 12, no. 1 (January 9, 2020): 183, https://doi.org/10.3390/nu12010183; De Vries, Vossen, and van der Kolk – van der Boom, "Social Media and Body Dissatisfaction."

TIPS FOR BUILDING A POSITIVE BODY IMAGE

- → Be aware of how you're interacting with social media.
- → Pay attention to which accounts or types of content trigger negative thoughts.
- → Understand digital distortion. "A Selfie" on YouTube is a short film by the Dove Self-Esteem Project. It reveals the posing, camera angles, special light, filters, and more that people go through to get the perceived perfect shot.
- → Look for ways to use social media in a positive way to interact and lift people up.
- → Be selective with your social media accounts. Unfollow accounts that trigger negative body image thoughts; instead focus on accounts that inspire you.
- → Journaling—use a journal to write down accomplishments and moments that make you proud. Keeping track of them can be a great tool for reflecting on your progress.
- → Avoid comparing yourself to others—you can do this by shifting focus from comparing yourself to others to personal growth and improvement. Record personal goals and track your progress over time. Celebrate your achievements regardless of how they compare to others'. For example, "I ran a personal best in the 800 today!" or "I stepped up to be a team leader. I'm excited to be a mentor to the younger runners."
- → Reframe negative thoughts about your body or your performance. For example, if you think, "I'm not going to be able to complete this race," consider reframing to "I'm getting stronger every day with practice, and I will do my best during this race."

- Practice positive self-talk—use affirmations like these:
  - I am strong and capable.
  - My body is powerful and helps me achieve my goals.
  - I am proud of my progress and effort.
  - I have the energy and endurance to finish this run.
  - I am exactly where I need to be right now.
  - I'm working hard and improving every run.
  - I'm rooting for myself.
- Take time to appreciate what your body can do. Celebrate accomplishments, like running a new distance or mastering a new technique. Recognize daily strengths, like doing well in school and doing your best at practice, eating well, and prioritizing sleep and recovery. These are other great additions for your journal.
- Respect your body by setting health-focused goals, such as remembering to bring your post-workout snack or fueling well at lunch to power you through your afternoon workout.

If you are struggling with body dissatisfaction even after incorporating some of these techniques, reach out to your parent or someone in your support system, like a school counselor, to help guide you through the best next steps.

DISORDERED EATING AND EATING DISORDERS

You may be hearing the terms disordered eating and eating disorders used interchangeably, but it's essential to understand they represent two different concepts. This understanding is important to apply the correct diagnosis and appropriate treatments.

DISORDERED EATING

Disordered eating refers to a wide range of behaviors that involve eating in a way that prevents full participation in life activities or impairs healthy growth and development. Signs may include:

- → Obsessive thoughts about food or weight
- → Struggling to eat in front of others
- → Fad dieting
- → Skipping meals and following a restrictive diet

Physical symptoms may include chronic stomach or GI issues, dry skin, brittle nails, feeling cold all the time, and depression. If left untreated, disordered eating can lead to an eating disorder, as noted by Jordana Tobelem, RD, LDN:

"As a registered dietitian who has worked extensively with the eating disorder community, I've seen firsthand how early intervention and support can make all the difference. Recognizing the signs of disordered eating and seeking help can prevent more severe health issues down the line. As trainers, coaches, and parents, it's important to foster an environment where young athletes feel empowered to nourish their bodies rather than restrict them, understanding that food is not the enemy, but rather a tool for performance and well-being."

EATING DISORDERS

An eating disorder is a clinically diagnosable mental health condition. As recognized in the Diagnostic Manual DSM-5

(*Diagnostic and Statistical Manual of Mental Disorders*)—they are characterized by severe disturbances in eating behaviors and related thoughts and emotions.

There are three common types of eating disorders: anorexia nervosa (AN), bulimia nervosa (BN), and binge eating disorder (BED).

ANOREXIA NERVOSA (AN)

AN is characterized by restricting what you eat, having a fear of gaining weight, and a distorted body image. Examples of behavior associated with AN may be avoiding meals, skipping breakfast, counting calories, and limiting foods one believes to be high in calories, like sweets, bread, and fats. Additionally, one's weight may increase, in turn triggering anxiety. So even with a lack of energy, the individual will still engage in excessive exercise. Oftentimes, a distorted body image will accompany AN, where the person sees themself as overweight, despite size and will spend time criticizing their body, unable to hear compliments from others.

BULIMIA NERVOSA (BN)

BN is an eating disorder characterized by recurrent episodes of binge eating, where large amounts of food are consumed in a short period, followed by behaviors to prevent weight gain, such as self-induced vomiting, misuse of laxatives, fasting, or excessive exercise. Individuals with bulimia often experience feelings of guilt, shame, and lack of control over their eating behaviors, which can significantly impact their physical health, including electrolyte imbalances, dental issues, and gastrointestinal problems, as well as their psychological well-being, often co-occurring with other mental health conditions like depression or anxiety.

BINGE EATING DISORDER (BED)

BED is an eating disorder characterized by recurrent episodes of consuming large amounts of food in a short period while feeling a lack of control over eating during these episodes. Unlike bulimia nervosa, individuals with BED do not regularly engage in compensatory behaviors such as purging or excessive exercise to prevent weight gain. Feelings of guilt, shame, and distress often accompany binge-eating episodes. BED can lead to significant physical health concerns such as obesity, high blood pressure, diabetes, and gastrointestinal issues, as well as psychological challenges, including depression, anxiety, and low self-esteem.

RESOURCES FOR LEARNING MORE ABOUT EATING DISORDERS

→ www.nationaleatingdisorders.org (NEDA)
NEDA has an online screening tool appropriate for ages 13 and up as well as resources for educators and families.

→ https://www.eatingdisorderhope.com
Eating Disorder Hope™ is an online community that offers resources, education, support, and inspiration to those struggling with anorexia nervosa, bulimia nervosa, binge eating disorder, body image issues, and a myriad of other disordered eating behaviors.

THE FEMALE AND MALE ATHLETE TRIADS

The female athlete triad and the male athlete triad represent three aspects of your physiology: energy availability, hormonal function, and bone mineral density.[51] In chapter 1, we discussed the importance of building a solid foundation by supporting the needs of your adolescent bone growth and mineral density. Just as the structural integrity of a house depends on a sturdy framework and quality materials, your body's strength and resilience rely on the balance and health of these physiological systems.

Energy Availability. In chapter 2, we discussed the concepts of metabolism and the feeling of "hitting the wall" during a run—the feeling when your body is not getting enough power and when you can't run another step. Repeated instances of feeling like this, multiple times of "going to the well" for resources that result in depleting your energy stores without properly refilling the tank can lead to low energy availability; more on this in the next section.

Menstrual Function. If you are not taking in enough energy, physiological functions like your menstrual cycle can be impacted when the production of hormones that regulate the cycle is interrupted. The loss of menstrual function is called amenorrhea. There are two types of amenorrhea. Primary amenorrhea is the delayed onset of the first menstrual period.

51 Marc A. Raj, Julie A. Creech, and Alan D. Rogol, "Female Athlete Triad," PubMed (Treasure Island, FL): StatPearls Publishing, 2020), https://www.ncbi.nlm.nih.gov/books/NBK430787.

Secondary amenorrhea is the absence of three or more consecutive menstrual cycles in a woman who previously had a regular cycle.

Bone Mineral Density. This is affected by both energy availability and menstrual function. Estrogen is essential for bone health, but it decreases in a disrupted menstrual cycle. In combination with inadequate nutrition, this can lead to low BMD.

KEY DIFFERENCES

In females, menstrual dysfunction is a clear indication of hormonal imbalance. In males, hormonal imbalance is less commonly diagnosed, with less awareness and absence of apparent indicators.

SIGNS OF THE TRIADS AND SIGNS OF LEA

FOR FEMALES:

- → Irregular periods
- → Amenorrhea
- → Stress fractures/Bone stress injuries
- → Delayed healing
- → Osteopenia/Osteoporosis (this would be diagnosed by a doctor through medical imaging)

FOR MALES:

- → Decreased testosterone (this would be diagnosed by a doctor through bloodwork)
- → Reduced muscle mass and strength
- → Increased body fat
- → Decreased bone density
- → Decreased libido

OTHER FACTORS BESIDES EATING DISORDERS THAT CONTRIBUTE TO THE TRIADS

An eating disorder or nutrition habits are not the only factors that may bring an athlete into the cycle of the triad. What factors might impact the development of the female or male athlete triad? Exercise patterns, psychological aspects, personality, social pressure, sleep, and recovery.

EXERCISE PATTERNS

As discussed, LEA and eating disorders are related to exercise patterns. For example, if your training volume increases and you don't respond with increased nutrition intake and adequate rest and recovery, this can lead to over-use injuries. Recent science shows that early specialization—focusing on a single sport from a young age—can also increase the risk of over-use injuries.[52]

PSYCHOLOGICAL ASPECTS/SOCIAL PRESSURE

The psychological component includes messaging that a certain body weight or shape determines performance. Coaches, peers, and parents may unintentionally promote an unhealthy focus on weight and appearance. This and the media glorifying thinness are both at the crux of the problem[53]—coaches, please see ideas for promoting a healthy running program in chapter 5. Parents, please read on to chapter 6 for additional information on conversations around nutrition at home.

---

52 Neeru Jayanthi et al., "Sports Specialization in Young Athletes," *Sports Health: A Multidisciplinary Approach* 5, no. 3 (October 25, 2013): 251–57, https://doi.org/10.1177/1941738112464626.

53 Koulanova et al., "Ideas for Action: Exploring Strategies to Address Body Image Concerns."

PERSONALITY

You may naturally have a high drive for achievement or perfection. This can cause you to push beyond healthy limits by ignoring signs of fatigue, injury, stress, and anxiety—this psychological stress can influence eating habits and menstrual function. Teammates, coaches, and parents can be supportive in watching for signs that a young runner's natural sense of achievement is putting them at risk.

SLEEP AND RECOVERY

The other pillar of strong recovery and preparedness for training is adequate sleep. Studies have shown that sleep deprivation in adolescent athletes is associated with an increased risk of musculoskeletal injury and a decline in cognitive performance. The recommended minimum amount of sleep for individuals between the ages of 7 and 19 is eight to nine hours per night.

RESOURCES FOR LEARNING MORE ABOUT THE FEMALE AND MALE ATHLETE TRIADS

The Female and Male Athlete Triad Coalition, a non-profit 501(c)(3) organization, represents vital medical, nursing, athletic, and sports medicine groups and concerned individuals who promote optimal health and well-being for athletes and active individuals.

https://femaleandmaleathletetriad.org.

A STORY OF UNINTENTIONAL UNDER-FUELING

Athletics was in my blood. My family lived and breathed it. My mom was a dedicated marathon runner, and my dad and brother raced bikes competitively. In our household, it wasn't a question of whether we would be outside; it was just a matter of what sport we'd be doing. From an early age, my days were spent sweating, pushing limits, and thriving in the spirit of competition.

In seventh grade, I found myself gravitating toward water polo. There wasn't a girls' team then, but that didn't stop me. I joined the boys' team, ready to prove I could hold my own. I dove in—literally—with everything I had. I trained relentlessly, determined not just to keep up but to excel.

Five years later, my persistence paid off. I managed to get women's water polo sanctioned as an official high school sport, a moment that felt like the culmination of my hard work and passion. By then, I was deep into a grueling training regimen: four hours a day split between morning swims before school and intense afternoon practices. On top of that, I started lifting weights with my dad, determined to grow stronger.

By my senior year, however, the demands of my athletic life began to take their toll. After six years of non-stop water polo and swimming, the burnout hit. I craved a fresh challenge, so I turned to cross-country. It seemed like a natural fit, and soon, I found myself building a routine around running. My days became a blur of activity: swimming from 5 to 7 a.m. , lifting weights during lunch, cross-country practice from 3 to 5 p.m., and water polo from 5 to 7 p.m.

I was pushing my body to its limits, but I loved it. I thrived on the challenge and the adrenaline.

My parents, both athletes themselves, kept my meals balanced and nutritious. They sent me to school with cash, ensuring I had what I needed to refuel. But I wasn't eating nearly enough for the intensity I was sustaining. I didn't notice it at first, but my body was crying for rest and recovery, and I wasn't allowing it. My parents didn't notice either. I was having too much fun, and so were they.

The shift came gradually. By the end of my senior year, I had lost more weight than I realized. I dropped to a precariously low number for my 5'8" frame. My energy levels plummeted, and soon, my menstrual cycle stopped. Blackouts became more frequent, my body teetering on the edge of collapse.

Ironically, it was a school project that made me confront reality. I was taking a class in preparation for studying physical therapy, and part of my coursework involved underwater weighing to determine body fat percentage. The result was startling: 6.2%. I was in trouble, and I couldn't ignore it any longer.

Once the fall sports season ended, I made a choice that ultimately saved me. I reduced my training volume by quitting water polo and swimming, and focused on nutrition intake that would support my running and strength training. Slowly but surely, my body began to heal. My menstrual cycle returned, I regained the weight I had lost, and I learned to listen to the needs of my body rather than push it to its breaking point.

The journey was far from over, but that turning point marked the start of a new chapter—a shift toward balance, recovery, and a deeper understanding of what it means to be strong.

—Lindsay, cyclist and runner

LOW ENERGY AVAILABILITY (LEA)

In chapter 2 and in this chapter's section on the triads, we discussed the concepts of metabolism and the feeling of "hitting the wall" during a run. The common thread between the nutrition challenges discussed in this chapter is LEA. Just like your custom-built house needs energy via electricity to run efficiently, your body needs energy (nutrition) for daily activities and exercise. When the house has a sufficient energy supply to meet all its basic needs, everything runs smoothly—the lights work, the heating and cooling systems work, appliances function correctly, and the house remains comfortable and well-maintained.

LEA occurs when you are not fueling enough to support your resting metabolic rate and the energy expended during exercise.[54] It's like trying to run your house on half the electricity it needs—the lights flicker, the heating and cooling systems struggle, and the appliances don't work properly. Due to the intuitive, intelligent system of your body, it will start making physiological adaptations to conserve energy, such as reducing metabolic rate, impairing reproductive functions, and decreasing bone maintenance. The body will prioritize vital organs and functions, reducing to less critical systems like reproductive health and bone maintenance. Insufficient energy can lead to deterioration in your house. In the body, it can lead to hormone imbalance, menstrual irregularities in females, and low testosterone in males. Inadequate energy for bone remod-

54 Bronwen Lundy et al., "Screening for Low Energy Availability in Male Athletes: Attempted Validation of LEAM-Q," *Nutrients* 14, no. 9 (April 29, 2022): 1873, https://doi.org/10.3390/nu14091873.

eling leads to low bone mineral density, and an energy deficit affects physical performance, immune function, and psychological well-being. All these signs and symptoms are found under the umbrella of REDs.

SIGNS OF LOW ENERGY AVAILABILITY

Feeling Very Tired: More than just the usual tiredness after running.

Weight Loss: Losing weight without trying or having trouble keeping healthy.

Frequent Sickness: Getting colds or other illnesses more often than usual.

Feeling Cold: Always feeling cold, even when others are comfortable.

ADDITIONAL CONSIDERATION

LEAF-Q for females and LEAM-Q for males are screening tools in development that focus on gender-specific physiological symptoms of insufficient energy intake. If you suspect you may be suffering from low energy availability, discuss it with your family and coaches so they can work together to find you the right sports doctor or registered sports dietitian for your needs.

REDs

REDs stands for relative energy deficiency in sports and is defined as "a syndrome of impaired physiological and/or psychological functioning experienced by female and male athletes that is caused by exposure to problematic (prolonged and/or severe) LEA."[55] The detrimental outcomes include, but are not limited to, decreases in energy metabolism, reproductive function, musculoskeletal health, immunity, glycogen synthesis, and cardiovascular and hematological health, which can all individually and synergistically lead to impaired well-being, increased injury risk, and decreased sports performance. The consequences amplify over time, making them increasingly challenging to repair. Prevention and early identification are critical factors in mitigating these outcomes.

Early indicators of REDs include:

→ Frequently ill or injured
→ Adapting poorly to training
→ Low moods or energy
→ Reluctant to rest or eat more
→ Preoccupation with food or body
→ Denial about a possible issue

For treatment and diagnosis, contact a medical professional that is trained in REDs or a registered sports dietitian with experience in treating REDs.

Resources for Learning More about REDs:

→ https://red-s.com
Project REDs' mission is to raise awareness of relative energy deficiency in sports through education, advocacy, and support.

55 Margo Mountjoy et al., "2023 International Olympic Committee's (IOC) Consensus Statement on Relative Energy Deficiency in Sport (REDs)," *British Journal of Sports Medicine* 57, no. 17 (September 1, 2023): 1073–97, https://doi.org/10.1136/bjsports-2023-106994.

→ https://www.redinsport.org
RED in Sport's mission is to educate athletes, coaches, medical professionals, parents, and supporters by advancing knowledge of REDs and providing a space for open, honest dialogue surrounding prevention, recovery, and support for all athletes.

SUPPORTING YOUR TEAMMATES

One of the unique aspects of cross-country and track and field is being a part of a team, building camaraderie, establishing identity, learning to recognize each other's strengths and weaknesses, and working to build each other up. You become pretty close, spending hours together at practice, team dinners, and meets, and it's hard not to notice when a teammate's behavior or habits change. This awareness is a casual observation and a responsibility we all share as teammates. For example, your teammate, the one full of energy and enthusiasm, becomes more withdrawn and seems tired at practice. At first, you might think it's the stress of school or lack of sleep, but you start to notice that they are having a difficult time executing workouts at practices, and at lunch, it seems they are pushing their food around their plate more than they are eating. You're concerned for your teammates and feel you should talk with them, but you fear it being awkward or upsetting them. Here is an example of a positive exchange that could happen between teammates:

"Hey Kate, are you okay? You seem tired lately," Jennifer asked kindly.

Kate's face looked anxious, and she looked away. "I'm just trying to get faster," she replied. "I need to lose a few pounds to improve my time."

Jennifer felt nervous to say more, but she knew about eating disorders and had learned the signs as well. She feared that Kate might struggle with something more severe than a desire to improve running times. She knew she needed to speak up and help her teammate.

"I'm concerned about you, Kate. I think talking to someone might help. We all want to see you healthy—we need your energy on this team."

Jennifer spoke with empathy, and Kate agreed to talk with their coach. Their coach was understanding and became involved in helping Kate find the right professional who could help with the underlying issues that led to her path toward an eating disorder.

PREVENTION AND MANAGEMENT STRATEGIES

Treatment of these nutritional challenges involves a multidisciplinary approach. Proper nutrition and consuming enough calories to match energy expenditure are crucial. The above information educates athletes, coaches, and healthcare providers on the signs and risks of LEA and the triads. Depending on the individual and challenge(s), nutrition counseling, medical intervention, and psychological support may be a part of the treatment plan. Here, you understand the nutritional challenges you may face in your running career, how they are related, what signs to look for, and how to seek help if you are struggling. Whether you are a runner, the coach, or a parent helping a young runner, I encourage you to read on. The next chapter, "Integrating Nutrition Education into Running Programs," is written for the coach, but since we're a team here, runners and parents—ask your coaches for nutrition education and offer to get involved in helping organize. Remember, your involvement can significantly impact these young runners' lives. If we're all working on helping these young runners build their custom homes, they will be formidable on and off the track.

CHAPTER FIVE

INTEGRATING NUTRITION EDUCATION INTO YOUR RUNNING PROGRAM

We don't accomplish anything in this world alone ... and whatever happens is the result of the whole tapestry of one's life and all the weavings of individual threads from one to another that creates something.

—Sandra Day O'Connor

Hi, coaches! In the first four chapters of this book, I wrote to the young runner, asking them to visualize their body as a one-of-a kind house, custom built to their unique physiology. We've used this analogy to look at what is happening in their body during this phase of their life and how, with nutrition, they can support the demands of growth and development and performance and recovery in running. While I wrote it for and to the young runners in your program, by now you probably know that I am passionate about getting the whole team of people around these young runners involved: you—their coach, their trainers, and parents or guardians.

It's exciting to be at the beginning of a young runner's career. You are most likely a runner yourself and you, too, have a story of how you grew with the sport. You can play the role of the interior designer so to speak. Just like a house isn't complete without proper furnishings, a running program isn't fully equipped without solid nutrition principles. However, many programs do not have the financial resources to bring in a sports nutritionist to talk with the team. And you may already feel stretched with bringing up new runners, organizing volunteers, writing plans that make sense for your individual runners, motivating, scheduling practices, registering for races, and more.

But the goal of maintaining normal growth and development—not just looking at performance results, but playing a role in developing strong, resilient runners—is the cornerstone of change. While I emphasize ownership for the runners in creating their own nutrition plans, your support and guidance can be the key to successfully integrating these principles into their training. Just as a well-furnished house provides comfort and functionality, your involvement in their nutrition education can provide the final touch that elevates their performance and well-being.

The following are what I call non-negotiables in incorporating nutrition education into your program. Throughout the chapter, you'll find tips on how to talk with a runner if you suspect that they might be going down a path of disordered eating or struggling with other nutritional challenges, as well as resources for further reading and education. For details on navigating nutritional challenges, please see chapter 4.

PERSONAL STATEMENT

As a mental health professional and psychology researcher with extensive experience in adolescent psychology, I use evidence-based strategies to help adolescents build resilience and develop a positive self-concept.

Utilizing strategies from recent research on body image and eating disorders, particularly those outlined in chapters 5 and 6, is crucial for enhancing body satisfaction and overall well-being. These approaches help athletes appreciate their bodies for their abilities, thereby boosting their confidence and performance.

This research is particularly valuable for young runners, as it addresses the pressures of competitive sports and societal standards. Integrating these strategies fosters both mental and physical health, enhancing their overall experience and success in athletics.

—Ashley Ford (psychology researcher & mental health professional)

ESTABLISH BASIC PRINCIPLES FOR YOUR TEAM LEADERS

Eating disorders do not discriminate. Eating disorders can develop in anyone. When looking at your young runners, all genders, races, sexual identities, and body shapes should be considered as athletes who could adopt an unhealthy relationship with food. As a coach, you have a tremendous responsibility and a gift to potentially change the trajectory of someone's life. I suggest setting aside time to have a pre-season meeting with your coaching team, including assistant coaches and athletic trainers, to discuss the following principles.

PRINCIPLE ONE: TAKE STEPS TO PROMOTE POSITIVE BODY IMAGE AND PREVENT A CULTURE OF DISORDERED EATING WITHIN YOUR TEAM

Research shows that physical activity generally promotes a positive body image and overall well-being; however, there are complexities in how exercise interacts with body image, especially concerning the risk of developing eating disorders. It is recommended that a balanced approach be found in exercise and body image to mitigate the risk of negative outcomes such as disordered eating.[56] So how can you support young runners in building positive body image?

POSITIVE COMMUNICATION

Instill the message in your coaching staff that lower body weight does not equal improved performance. An undernourished runner can lose muscle and experience decreased performance.[57] See signs of disordered eating to look for on page 103.

---

56 Melissa Rizk et al., "Physical Activity in Eating Disorders: A Systematic Review," *Nutrients* 12, no. 1 (January 9, 2020): 183, https://doi.org/10.3390/nu12010183.

57 Silvia Sánchez-Díaz et al., "Effects of Nutrition Education Interventions in Team Sport Players. A Systematic Review," *Nutrients* 12, no. 12 (November 28, 2020): 3664, https://doi.org/10.3390/nu12123664.

POSITIVE REINFORCEMENT

There is great value in encouraging supportive and positive reinforcement. You can use verbal praise, such as, "I'm really impressed with how you executed that 400. I can tell how much dedication you have," or, "You did a great job handling that shove from the other runner in the race. Keep up the good work." Let your runners know that they're always producing results with praise like, "Your effort and improvement are inspiring. You should be proud of yourself."

Supportive gestures like high-fives, or a supportive handshake after a race or practice, also go a long way. Ask your athletes what their preference is when it comes to physical support, some may prefer a high five, others a special handshake or others may not prefer physical support at all.

When giving immediate feedback, make sure to keep it positive and helpful.

- → **Prompt correction:** "Great effort on that mile. Let's practice being more conservative in the first 800 and see how that works for you."
- → **Quick praise:** "You did great! This is working for you—let's keep at it!"
- → **Real-time guidance:** "Focus on your breathing in this next lap."

Focus on performance/skill as opposed to how a runner looks. For example, "Great job bringing your pre-run snack today, you executed a great practice," as opposed to, "You were looking lean and fast today."

Or conversely, "I'm sorry you felt fatigued today; let's try a pre-workout snack tomorrow to ensure your glycogen stores are topped off," as opposed to, "You might be feeling better if you lost a couple pounds."

Celebrate the whole runner. Take an interest in their performance on the track and in the classroom. Support their interest in healthy activities outside of running.

Consider Further Body Confidence Education

There are a few very positive and effective resources to help explain and inform you and your runners on body confidence:

- → **The Body Positive:** A non-profit organization offering tools and resources for promoting body positivity.
- → **The Dove Self-Esteem Project:** Offers educational resources and programs to help improve self-esteem and body image in young people.
- → **Eating Disorder Hope™:** Comprehensive resources and support for those dealing with body image issues and eating disorders.

PRINCIPLE TWO: ESTABLISH A PROTOCOL FOR PRE-SEASON RUNNING-SPECIFIC NUTRITION EDUCATION

In your meeting with your coaching staff and trainers, establish how running-specific nutrition education will happen. It's important that the protocols are specific to your sport; your young runners need to be and will be fueling differently than the football team. You have options for how to facilitate nutrition education. Scan the QR code to find the courses and materials developed to complement this book, including a curriculum for delivering nutrition education to your team, or you can hire a local sports nutritionist to talk with the team. The Academy of Nutrition and Dietetics (https://www.eatright.

org/) has a search tool for nutritionists in your area, where you can also filter by specialty.

Pre-season training seems a logical time to set up this learning time; it allows your runners to start practicing what nutrition protocols are working for them as an individual and for you to have established goals for the team before the racing season starts. *The Young Runner's Guide to Nutrition* curriculum learning can happen in person, over Zoom, or be self-guided. Invite trainers and parents to participate in learning. See page 100 for a sample email to parents.

Here are *The Young Runner's Guide to Nutrition* curriculum highlights:

- → Each module has interactive and critical thinking exercises for your runners to participate in. In-person or Zoom lessons can be combined into a couple of longer sessions or could be broken up over a few days' time—taking time before or after a training session to sit down and "discover" together.
- → The modules can stand alone or they can be used in conjunction with your athletes having a copy of the book. Even if your team is reading the book, setting aside lesson time to discuss what they've read will help the principles discussed to sink in. It gives the runners an opportunity to ask questions and for there to be collective learning.

For in-person learning, I encourage personal anecdotes. Do you, the coach, have a personal story around nutrition that you would like to share? Regardless of whether or not you have a nutrition background, I think it's important to explain that we are operating off of what the science currently states; this could evolve, but for now we're using it to establish a launching pad from which to start helping the athletes in building nutrition habits that will allow them to grow and develop and continue their running career long into the future.

The modules in *The Young Runner's Guide to Nutrition* curriculum include:

Module One. Navigating Adolescence: Understanding Your Unique Physiology. This module highlights the growth and development of the adolescent body and how proper nutrition can help keep hormones in balance and support athletes' bone health and muscle development, and boost their brain and cognitive development. It also discusses how all of these physiological aspects relate to their running now and how they can impact their future. Interactive questions and quizzes include a reflection on their current nutrition intake, as well as discussion time with a partner (if applicable) around what nutrition changes can support bone and muscle development; making connections between nutrients and what types of foods they come from, and more.

Module Two. Optimizing Nutrition for Performance and Recovery. The module reviews the essential nutrients—macronutrients and micronutrients. Hydration is discussed in detail, as well as key concepts like metabolism and energy availability. The topic of supplementation is also covered. Interactive questions and quizzes include calculating individual carbohydrate intake needs, strategizing how to stay properly hydrated, and discussion around supplements.

Module Three. Strategic Fueling and Hydration. This module covers how your runners can strategically plan their nutrition to provide their body with the nutrients it needs to keep their minds sharp in the classroom, to perform in their workouts and races, and to recover quickly. Topics include pre-workout nutrition, during-workout nutrition, and post-run nutrition as well as sample timelines for fueling throughout their training and competition days.

Module Four. Navigating Nutritional Challenges. In this module we cover several nutritional challenges including low energy availability, disordered eating, eating disorders including anorexia nervosa, bulimia nervosa, binge eating disorder, the female and male athlete triads, and REDs. Participants will leave understanding the signs and symptoms of each, prevention and management strategies, and resources for learning more.

Module Five. Family Support: Fueling Together. In the final module we discuss concepts and ideas for how to support the unique demands of your family. We'll explore tips for how to plan for the week, how to include the whole family in food preparation, and how to foster open communication around nutrition. Included is a review of the first four modules; reminders for how coaches, parents, and athletes can continue to foster a healthy running community around their team; and a list of global resources for continued learning or seeking help, if needed.

DEAR PARENTS, GUARDIANS, AND ATHLETES

We are excited for the cross-country [or track] season and are thrilled that you are a part of the team and participating in pre-season training [if applicable]. We are excited to provide nutrition education in our program. We will kick off five weeks of Nutrition Sessions on XX. They will be held after practice on Thursdays at X:XX. We will keep the sessions to 1 hour or less. The length may depend on how many questions are fielded and what discussions arise from the session. We will be using the *The Young Runners Guide to Nutrition* curriculum to guide our learning. Please RSVP here:

Thank you for your participation,

Coach X

PRINCIPLE THREE: INCLUDE ONGOING REMINDERS THROUGHOUT THE SEASON

FOOD-FIRST APPROACH

The food-first approach is focused on obtaining essential nutrients from whole foods rather than supplements. Nutrition intake is from a balanced diet of fruits, vegetables, whole grains, lean proteins, and healthy fats. The complex mix of nutrients in whole foods, including vitamins, minerals, fiber, and antioxidants work together to support optimal health.

PRE-WORKOUT NUTRITION

The timing of a workout and the time elapsed since a runner's last meal are fundamental in planning pre-workout nutrition. If it's been more than 4 hours since a balanced meal, a mini-meal or snack before exercising reinforces the body's energy stores, providing a steady fuel supply for the workout. Mini meals might include whole-grain toast with peanut butter and banana slices or Homemade Granola and Yogurt Bowl (page 215), and a snack might be a No-Bake Energy Bar (page 211) or nuts and dried fruit.

DURING-WORKOUT NUTRITION

Regularly consuming simple carbohydrates during long workouts ensures that the body remains fueled, preventing energy depletion and keeping the runner performing at their best.

Like pre-run nutrition, the closer one is to the workout, the simpler the fuel needs to be. For workouts lasting more than 60 minutes, incorporating simple carbohydrates every 30 minutes will keep energy stores topped off. An example would be consuming a sports gel, a few sports chews, or a small piece of fruit every 30 minutes.

POST-WORKOUT NUTRITION

By consuming carbohydrates immediately after a workout, the body quickly replenishes glycogen stores. Proteins are essential for muscle repair and growth. A balanced post-workout snack could be a smoothie with carbohydrates and protein, a turkey sandwich, or a mix of nuts and fruit. Other options include a granola bar or pretzels paired with a sports drink.

PRINCIPLE FOUR: PROVIDE ADDITIONAL RACE DAY/WEEKEND NUTRITION SUPPORT

Team dinners are a great way to get the runners involved in the kitchen and to build camaraderie amongst the team. Again, an online sign-up like Sign-up Genius is a great way to get families to sign up to host. The hosts can still ask other families to contribute a meal, salad, or dessert to feed the group. You can find team dinner ideas in chapter 7.

Traveling for a meet may be one of the most challenging days or weekends to get nutrition right. See page 60 for sample fueling schedules for race days/weekends. As the coach, you may have control over where the team eats before, after, or even during competition. Take the time to research what is close to the hotel and/or venue and make a reservation in advance at a restaurant that will accommodate the various needs of your runners. Encourage them to bring their own food for the venue (see page 61), but also provide them a list of healthy alternatives in the area if they are able to leave the venue during competition.

HOW TO TALK WITH A YOUNG RUNNER ABOUT DISORDERED EATING

If you suspect a young runner you know is starting down a path of disordered eating or is presenting signs of an eating disorder, here's how you can navigate that.

RECOGNIZE SIGNS AND SYMPTOMS OF DISORDERED EATING IN ATHLETES

→ Dramatic weight loss or gain
→ Frequently talking about food and body image
→ Compulsive exercise habits—adding on to their workouts or not following protocol
→ Mention of exercising so they can eat and/or because of what they ate
→ Negative self-talk
→ Communicating distress when a workout is missed
→ Not eating in social situations like team dinners
→ Extra fatigue, dizziness, shortness of breath at workouts

What should you do if you see signs of disordered eating? First, address the problem early. The earlier an eating disorder is diagnosed, the better the chances for a full recovery. Then share your assessment with the athletic trainer, who can advise you on the school's protocol on disordered eating and guide you in the next steps.

STARTING THE CONVERSATION[58]

Starting a conversation with a young runner may feel overwhelming as the response is unknown. And it's true the athlete may deny that they have a problem or may feel defensive when they are approached. They, too, may be fearful of negative reactions if they open up or fearful of losing control over something they believe to be in control of. Here are some tips for preparing

58 Elisabeth (Lisette) Yorke, Tara Evans-Atkinson, and Debra K. Katzman, "Shared Language and Communicating with Adolescents and Young Adults with Eating Disorders," *Paediatrics & Child Health* 26, no. 1 (April 17, 2020), https://doi.org/10.1093/pch/pxaa047.

for the conversation and creating an environment where the athlete can open up.

Do your research. Have a list of qualified professionals in your area that you can refer your athlete to. Again, you can utilize the Academy of Nutrition and Dietetics (https://www.eatright.org) which has a search tool for nutritionists in your area where you can also filter by specialty.

Keep the conversation private. If talking with the runner, do so in a private setting that does not involve food where they will feel comfortable and safe. Simply express what you have observed and that you are concerned for them, using compassionate language that focuses on health and well-being rather than appearance or weight and conveys concern rather than judgment.

Be empathetic. Enter the conversation with the intent to understand, validate feelings, and be aware that there may be resistance.

Follow up. Set a time to follow up within a few days to a week. Follow the same protocol for a private setting. Share with them the resources you've gathered, like a list of professionals in your area, a copy of this book, or handouts from *The Young Runner's Guide to Nutrition* curriculum.

Example conversation

Coach: "Hey, I've noticed you've been working hard lately. How has your energy been?"

Athlete: "I'm okay. Extra tired, maybe. Maybe not eating enough. I'm just trying to keep my weight down for races."

Coach: "I understand that performance is important to you. I'd like to suggest focusing on making sure your body feels strong and energized. Remember, fueling well is one of the best tools for good performance."

Athlete: "Yeah, I guess I haven't been eating as much to stay lighter."

Coach: "I understand you're being mindful, but instead of focusing on weight, we can set some goals around strength and endurance. How does that sound?"

Athlete: "I know. It's just hard to know exactly what to do, but I don't want to feel tired all of the time and not reach my potential."

Coach: "Agreed. Let's work together to make a plan to make sure you're feeling and performing your best. How about I do some homework and we'll set a time to meet next week?"

Athlete: "Sounds good, thank you for your support, coach."

FURTHER RESOURCES

→ The National Eating Disorders Association (NEDA) provides resources for body image and eating disorders, including support for coaches, such as NEDA's Coach and Trainer Toolkit.

→ Ongoing communication: Once your athlete is receiving the treatment they need that is specific to them, it's essential to continue to show your support and understanding.

Do's and Don'ts of continued communication (see Principle One):[59]

Do

- → Encourage dialogue—create an open environment that encourages athletes to come to you with concerns.
- → Use supportive language that focuses on health and well-being and fosters a positive environment.
- → Emphasize performance over appearance—praise athletes for their skills and effort, not their appearance.
- → Respect privacy and confidentiality—approach athletes privately if you notice new or continued signs of a nutritional challenge.

Don't

- → Don't comment on weight or body size.
- → Don't use weigh-ins as a measure of success.
- → Don't use negative comparisons—avoid comparing athletes to one another, especially regarding body size.
- → Don't underestimate your influence—respect the impact of your words and actions on athletes.

Books

- → *Running in Silence: My Drive for Perfection and the Eating Disorder That Fed It* by Rachel Steil
- → *Body Image: Understanding and Improving Body Image in Children and Adolescents* by Karen R. Koenig

---

59 Shelley L. Holden and Timothy M. Baghurst, "Ten Practical Strategies Coaches Can Use to Promote Nutrition to Their Athletes," *Strategies* 31, no. 6 (November 2, 2018): 34–41, https://doi.org/10.1080/08924562.2018.1515681; Sánchez-Díaz et al., "Effects of Nutrition Education Interventions."

CHAPTER SIX

FAMILY SUPPORT: FUELING TOGETHER

Cooking with kids is not just about ingredients, recipes, and cooking. It's about harnessing imagination, empowerment, and creativity.

—Guy Fieri

I grew up in a different time, just like you, in a home environment unique to my family. My parents were schoolteachers; as you've read, my dad was a coach. The schedule still allowed us to be home for dinner together most nights and for a home-cooked meal to be on the table. We ate together and talked about our days. The conversation didn't revolve around what we were eating, but coming from the Midwest, there was always a lean protein, grain, and vegetable on the table.

Growing up in that environment was like living in a well-built house. My parents' steady jobs and structured schedules strengthened the foundation. The walls were the routines and traditions that held us together, like having dinner as a family.

I took this for granted growing up and often asked myself how they did it once I was in the same position.

I, too, had a unique situation. Before my daughter started running, she played club soccer. Practices were often during the usual dinner hour, so it was a scramble to get in an after-school snack and then a quick bite before or during the carpool to practice. Dinner was often late when we were tired, and we usually ate in shifts and on the couch. The pandemic of 2020 gave us some gifts: more time together at home and more consistent dinner times. This gave me a different lens on the needs and habits of my teenage daughter, who was now running as her primary sport.

This is just my story. You have your own. Your house may look different—perhaps you're a single parent, a guardian, a family of two, or a family of six with children in multiple sports. As an adult, your nutritional needs differ from those of your growing young runner. How do you even begin to sort out all the information, work your job, care for your children and home, and get dinner on the table that meets everyone's needs?

This chapter discusses concepts and ideas for supporting your family's unique demands. We'll explore tips for planning for the week, including the whole family in food preparation, fostering open communication around nutrition, recognizing signs of eating disorders, and talking with your child about this challenging topic, along with guidance for seeking professional help.

The science shows us that making food choices is complex for adolescents, with influences from family, friends, and coaches.[60] Studies also show that adolescence is a critical time for your child to start gaining autonomy over what they eat.[61]

We are going to start with looking at meal planning, but please read on for more information on how to foster open communication around nutrition and guidance if you think your child may have or is developing signs of disordered eating or an eating disorder.

MEAL PLANNING

Prepare today. Conquer tomorrow.

—Unknown

Meal planning can reduce food costs[62] by allowing fewer meals to be grabbed on the go, ensure that your young runner is getting the balanced nutrition they need to excel in the classroom, on the track, and on the cross-country course, and reduce the stress of wondering what to make or eat.

We've established that each household is unique, and even with all this valuable information you might be wondering—

60 Sarah Snuggs and Kate Harvey, "Family Mealtimes: A Systematic Umbrella Review of Characteristics, Correlates, Outcomes, and Interventions," *Nutrients* 15, no. 13 (January 1, 2023): 2841, https://doi.org/10.3390/nu15132841; Isobel R. Contento, Sunyna S. Williams, John L. Michela, and Amie B. Franklin, "Understanding the Food Choice Process of Adolescents in the Context of Family and Friends," *Journal of Adolescent Health* 38, no. 5 (May 2006): 575–82. https://doi.org/10.1016/j.jadohealth.2005.05.025; Margo Mountjoy et al., "IOC Consensus Statement on Relative Energy Deficiency in Sport (RED-S): 2018 Update," *British Journal of Sports Medicine* 52, no. 11 (May 17, 2018): 687–97, https://doi.org/10.1136/bjsports-2018-099193.

61 Mountjoy et al., "IOC Consensus Statement."

62 "Meal Prep Guide," *The Nutrition Source*, October 2, 2020, https://nutritionsource.hsph.harvard.edu/meal-prep.

where do I start? The key to success is in planning as a household unit. So here are some first steps.

CREATE A FOOD SHOPPING LIST

Establish a weekly day and time to select recipes for the week. Utilize the young runner's pantry, refrigerator, and freezer list (page 127) to have staples already in the house—grains, canned goods, baking products, oils, spices, and pantry and refrigerator grab-and-go snacks. Once these essentials are in your house, weekly shopping will be easier.

Having a grocery list posted somewhere in a shared space that household members can add to when they use the last of an item is a great way to keep everyone involved in meal planning. You may consider using a shared app like AnyList (anylist.com) to create shopping lists and share from your devices.

PRE-SELECT RECIPE CHOICES

Provide those participating in meal planning with a list of recipe choices to prompt ideas for the week. I recommend selecting a limited number of recipes to start:

- → One portable weekday breakfast (Waffle Breakfast Sandwich)
- → One smoothie (Berry Power Smoothie)
- → One weekend breakfast (The Best Banana Pancakes)
- → Two portable snacks (one savory and one sweet—like the Egg Muffin Cups and No-Bake Energy Bar)
- → Three weekday dinners that can also be used for lunch leftovers (Roast Chicken with Root Vegetables, Tofu Buddha Bowl, Spaghetti Bake)

- One weekday lunch not made from leftovers (White Bean and Avocado Wrap with Chipotle Slaw)
- One weekend dinner (Thai Green Curry with Chicken and Sweet Potatoes)
- The weekend dinner could be a meal that is a bit more time intensive, but that also results in leftovers for lunch.
- One evening snack (The Ultimate Oatmeal Raisin Cookie and Yogurt)

ESTABLISH THE DAY FOR GROCERY SHOPPING

On a calendar, establish the official grocery shopping day, and do your best to involve those who will be helping with the meal preparation. It may be best to do this the same day as creating the list, as they have already scheduled out time to be a part of the planning.[63] Write down when you'll prepare and eat which meals, so if you're eating in shifts, everyone understands the flow of the week.

SET A DAY/TIME FOR ONE OR MORE FAMILY MEALS

We so often think about family dinner as the time to gather, but as we discussed, so many families are dispersed, doing their own activities at this time. I spent too much time beating myself up over this. It was liberating to find a meal time that worked for us. I had a friend in Seattle who would purposefully set aside breakfast time with her son. It was a meal that was important to him and that he enjoyed—it was a special time for

63 Bri DeRosa, "How to Balance Kid Sports and Family Dinner," The Family Dinner Project, July 25, 2022, https://thefamilydinnerproject.org/blog/how-to-balance-kid-sports-and-family-dinner.

them to bond—whether they were having a conversation or not. It set a positive and caring tone for the day for both of them.

BE FLEXIBLE

There will most likely be a night in the week where doing takeout makes sense. As best you can, establish that day and choose a meal that provides the three macronutrients. Pizza is great for this. And a salad at home can come together in minutes.

SELECT A COOLER SPECIFICALLY FOR THE CAR

You may not have time to stop at home before practice, or you have hungry and thirsty kids after practice, and you still have an hour of carpool. Pack pre- and post-workout snacks and drinks in the car.[64]

INVOLVE YOUR YOUNG RUNNER

You can even assign tasks. Ask them questions like: What meal or snack are you most looking forward to? Would you like to prepare that meal? Would you like to chop vegetables, or make rice or quinoa? This allows them to get involved in the way that is most meaningful for them. Give opportunities to change or evolve.[65]

---

64 Sarah Kinsella, "Sports Nutrition for Busy Families and Busy Lifestyles," HealthyChildren.org, n.d., https://www.healthychildren.org/English/healthy-living/nutrition/Pages/Sports-Nutrition-for-Busy-Families-and-Busy-Lifestyles.aspx.

65 Amanda M. Ziegler et al., "An Ecological Perspective of Food Choice and Eating Autonomy among Adolescents," *Frontiers in Psychology* 12 (April 21, 2021), https://doi.org/10.3389/fpsyg.2021.654139.

Invite them to prepare their lunch for the next day, the night before. Allow yourself and your young runner time to get into the new rhythm; if you have a day or week that doesn't go smoothly, give yourself and your young runner some grace and start fresh the following week.

START SMALL

If all of this looks very different from how you operate, start small.[66] Pick just one breakfast, snack, lunch, and dinner for the week (or less); if that feels like too much, give your family time to find the types of meals and the rhythm of planning and meal preparation that works for you. It may need to be a different day each week to accommodate schedules. If this is the case, perhaps pick a time each week to look ahead at the next week and schedule your family meeting and meal preparation time.

Here are two sample meal plans with tips on when and how to prepare the meals. Following these protocols will help you get into a rhythm for creating your plans. I've separated the weekday from the weekend, as the schedule will likely look different.

66 Bri DeRosa, "How to Balance Kid Sports and Family Dinner," The Family Dinner Project, July 25, 2022, https://thefamilydinnerproject.org/blog/how-to-balance-kid-sports-and-family-dinner.

SAMPLE PLAN 1

The weekend before the week starts, prepare:

- → Waffle Breakfast Sandwich
- → Almond Butter Banana Bread with Chocolate Chips and Walnuts
- → No-Bake Energy Bar
- → Pea Pesto Sauce
- → Pea Pesto Pasta Salad
- → Roast Chicken with Root Vegetables
- → Fudgy Chocolate Chia Pudding
- → Cook grains and chop vegetables and fruit

Midweek Prep:

- → **Tuesday night:** Prepare an easy dinner here, like the leftover Pea Pesto for Pesto Grilled Cheese paired with a salad or steamed vegetable. This allows for time to take the leftover chicken and turn it into Apple-Almond Chicken Salad for lunches
- → **Wednesday night:** Make the Tofu Buddha Bowl and Homemade Granola
- → **Friday night:** Make the Spaghetti Bake

Weekend Prep:

- → **Saturday:** Make Breakfast Burritos with Tots for breakfast that can also be used for breakfast or lunch the following week. Lunch on Saturday may be an excellent time for everyone to sit down and make the meal plan for the following week. Then shop on Saturday afternoon or Sunday morning.

- **Sunday:** Meal Prep Day to follow into Sample Plan 2
    - Homemade Granola
    - White Bean and Avocado Wraps with Chipotle Slaw
    - Power Breakfast Cookies
    - Thai Green Curry with Chicken and Sweet Potatoes
    - Homemade Granola

SAMPLE PLAN 1

	MONDAY	TUESDAY	WEDNESDAY	THURSDAY
BREAKFAST	Waffle Breakfast Sandwich	Waffle Breakfast Sandwich	Waffle Breakfast Sandwich	Waffle Breakfast Sandwich
SNACK	Almond Butter Banana Bread with Chocolate Chips and Walnuts	Almond Butter Banana Bread with Chocolate Chips and Walnuts	Almond Butter Banana Bread with Chocolate Chips and Walnuts	Almond Butter Banana Bread with Chocolate Chips and Walnuts
LUNCH	Pea Pesto Pasta Salad	Pea Pesto Pasta Salad	Apple-Almond Chicken Salad	Apple-Almond Chicken Salad
SNACK	No-Bake Energy Bar	No-Bake Energy Bar	No-Bake Energy Bar	No-Bake Energy Bar
DINNER	Leftover Roast Chicken and Vegetables	Pesto Grilled Cheese	Tofu Buddha Bowl	Tofu Buddha Bowl
SNACK	Fudgy Chocolate Chia Pudding	Fudgy Chocolate Chia Pudding	Fudgy Chocolate Chia Pudding	Fudgy Chocolate Chia Pudding

SAMPLE PLAN 1

	FRIDAY		SATURDAY	SUNDAY
BREAKFAST	Waffle Breakfast Sandwich	PRE-WORKOUT	Maple Banana Custard Oatmeal	Maple Banana Custard Oatmeal
SNACK	Almond Butter Banana Bread with Chocolate Chips and Walnuts	POST-WORKOUT	Smoothie of choice	Smoothie of choice
LUNCH	Leftover Tofu Buddha Bowl	BRUNCH	Breakfast Burritos with Tots	Breakfast Burritos with Tots
SNACK	No-Bake Energy Bar	SNACK	Almond Butter Banana Bread	Almond Butter Banana Bread
DINNER	Spaghetti Bake with a salad	DINNER	Spaghetti Bake with a salad	Thai Green Curry with Chicken and Sweet Potatoes
SNACK	Fudgy Chocolate Chia Pudding	SNACK	Homemade Granola and Yogurt Bowl	Homemade Granola and Yogurt Bowl

NOTES

SAMPLE PLAN 2

See Sunday meal prep at the end of Sample Week 1.

Midweek Prep:

- **Wednesday Night:** Keep dinner easy with the Weeknight Cast Iron Pizza so that you have time to prepare the lasagna. Prep the lasagna and bake that night or refrigerate to bake the following evening
- **Friday Night:** Make the Peanut Butter and Jam Overnight Oats for the weekend and they can also flow into the following week.

Weekend Prep:

- **Saturday:** The Best Banana Pancakes—these can be frozen and flow into the following week, too.
- **Sunday:** Meal Prep Day to flow into the following week
  - Sheet Pan Greek Turkey Meatballs and Vegetables with Lemony Rice
  - The Ultimate Oatmeal Raisin Cookie

SAMPLE PLAN 2

	MONDAY	TUESDAY	WEDNESDAY	THURSDAY
BREAKFAST	Breakfast Burrito with Tots	Breakfast Burrito with Tots	Breakfast Burrito with Tots	Breakfast Burrito with Tots
SNACK	Homemade Granola and Yogurt Bowl	Homemade Granola and Yogurt Bowl	Homemade Granola and Yogurt Bowl	Homemade Granola and Yogurt Bowl
LUNCH	White Bean and Avocado Wrap with Chipotle Slaw	White Bean and Avocado Wrap with Chipotle Slaw	White Bean and Avocado Wrap with Chipotle Slaw	Leftover Weeknight Cast Iron Pizza
SNACK	Power Breakfast Cookie and fruit	Power Breakfast Cookie and fruit	Power Breakfast Cookie and fruit	Power Breakfast Cookie and fruit
DINNER	Leftover Thai Green Curry with Chicken and Sweet Potatoes	Leftover Thai Green Curry with Chicken and Sweet Potatoes	Weeknight Cast Iron Pizza	Homestyle Lasagna with a salad
SNACK	Fudgy Chocolate Chia Pudding	Fudgy Chocolate Chia Pudding	Fudgy Chocolate Chia Pudding	Fudgy Chocolate Chia Pudding

SAMPLE PLAN 2

	FRIDAY		SATURDAY	SUNDAY
BREAKFAST	Breakfast Burrito with Tots	PRE-WORKOUT	Peanut Butter and Jam Overnight Oats	Peanut Butter and Jam Overnight Oats
SNACK	Homemade Granola and Yogurt Bowl	POST-WORKOUT	Smoothie of choice	Smoothie of choice
LUNCH	Leftover Weeknight Cast Iron Pizza	BRUNCH	The Best Banana Pancakes, 2 eggs	The Best Banana Pancakes, 2 eggs
SNACK	Power Breakfast Cookie and fruit	SNACK	Hummus and vegetables	Hummus and vegetables
DINNER	Homestyle Lasagna with a salad	DINNER	Leftovers or takeout	Sheet Pan Greek Turkey Meatballs and Vegetables with Lemony Rice
SNACK	Fudgy Chocolate Chia Pudding	SNACK	Fudgy Chocolate Chia Pudding	The Ultimate Oatmeal Raisin Cookie

FOSTERING HEALTHY CONVERSATION AROUND NUTRITION CHALLENGES

You've established a meal planning routine in your home, and you have involvement from your young runner, but this does not mean that they are immune to struggling with body image (page 72) or showing signs of disordered eating (page 76), or one of the other nutrition challenges discussed in chapter 4. Even with knowing the signs and symptoms and knowing that talking with them is the first step in getting the help they need, conversing with your young runner about your concerns might feel scary or overwhelming. Here are some ideas for how to navigate this delicate landscape.

RECOGNIZE THE SIGNS AND SYMPTOMS OF DISORDERED EATING IN YOUR YOUNG RUNNER[67]

You may notice signs at home that others outside the home might not notice as you more intimately see your young runner's habits and routines. You can also see signs and symptoms for coaches to look for in chapter 5:

→ Change in eating habits
→ Mood swings and increased irritability
→ Complaints of fatigue or physical symptoms, like a lost menstrual cycle for girls
→ Social withdrawal and isolation
→ Wearing baggy clothing

67 Psychology Today, "Parenting a Child with an Eating Disorder," 2024, https://www.psychologytoday.com/us/basics/eating-disorders/parenting-a-child-with-an-eating-disorder#how-should-i-prepare-for-a-conversation-about-my-childs-eating-disorder.

STARTING THE CONVERSATION[68]

Research resources. Part of supporting your young runner will be providing them with resources for education and therapy. The National Eating Disorders Association (NEDA) has an online screening tool appropriate for ages 13 and up. Psychologytoday.com has a comprehensive therapist search tool where you can specify your exact needs; for example—a female therapist specializing in eating disorders with teens, knowledgeable in sports performance, and with online availability.

Make a safe environment. Determine a safe, calm, confidential environment that does not involve food.

Be empathetic. Enter the conversation with the intent to understand and show a genuine interest in what they are experiencing. Simply express what you have observed and that you are concerned for them; using compassionate language that focuses on health and well-being rather than appearance or weight and conveys concern rather than judgment. Be aware that there may be resistance.

Follow up. If it does not happen in the first conversation, establish a time to follow-up and seek out the right treatment together.

ONGOING COMMUNICATION

Once your young runner is receiving the treatment they need that is specific to them, it's essential to continue to show your support and understanding. Adolescents with eating disorders

---

68 Elisabeth (Lisette) Yorke, Tara Evans-Atkinson, and Debra K Katzman, "Shared Language and Communicating with Adolescents and Young Adults with Eating Disorders," *Paediatrics & Child Health* 26, no. 1 (April 17, 2020), https://doi.org/10.1093/pch/pxaa047; *Psychology Today*, "Parenting a Child with an Eating Disorder."

may interpret feedback differently, and their disorder can influence their perception of comments.

- → Avoid implying fault

  Statement to avoid: "You need to stop focusing so much on your weight. This is all your fault for not eating right."

  Alternative: "I'm here to help you with your nutrition and overall health. Let's work together on finding what makes you feel good and strong."

- → Avoid blaming

  Statement to avoid: "If you just ate more normally, you wouldn't have these problems."

  Alternative: "It's important that we look at ways to make sure you're getting the right nutrients. We can explore some healthy eating habits together."

ORGANIZATIONS AND SUPPORT GROUPS

- → National Eating Disorders Association (NEDA)

  Resources for body image and eating disorders, including support for parents and coaches.

- → The Body Positive

  Non-profit organization offering tools and resources for promoting body positivity.

- → Eating Disorder Hope™

  Comprehensive resources and support for those dealing with body image issues and eating disorders.

- → The Dove Self-Esteem Project

  Educational resources and programs to help improve self-esteem and body image in young people.

BOOKS

- → *The Body Image Workbook for Teens: Activities to Help Girls Develop a Healthy Body Image in an Image-Obsessed World* by Julia V. Taylor
- → *The Self-Esteem Workbook for Teens: Activities to Help You Build Confidence and Achieve Your Goals* by Lisa M. Schab
- → *Body Image: Understanding and Improving Body Image in Children and Adolescents* by Karen R. Koenig
- → *The Mindful Teen: Powerful Skills to Help You Handle Stress One Moment at a Time* by Gina Biegel

In this chapter, we looked at how parents can influence their children's eating habits, the importance of developing autonomy around their food choices, and how to help facilitate this through conversation, meal planning, cooking, and eating together. In the final chapter, we get to start practicing everything we've learned so far, including recipes that meet the demands of your young runner's schedule. The chapter begins with what staples to have in your pantry, refrigerator, and freezer and tips for success in the kitchen. I trust these recipes will be a launching pad for how and when to incorporate your favorite family recipes into a routine that will meet your young runner's growth and development needs.

CHAPTER SEVEN

NUTRIENT-DENSE RECIPES

No one is born a great cook, one learns by doing.

—Julia Child

Finally—you get to start baking and cooking! I'm excited to share with you these recipes specially curated to a young runner's school and running schedule. We start with what staples to have in your pantry, refrigerator, and freezer. This list is based on the recipes in this book and also includes some additional grab-and-go snacks, such as graham crackers and pretzels. Read on for tips for success in the kitchen and instructions on how to successfully execute some cooking tasks, like pressing tofu and wrapping a burrito. Planning and cooking together is a great opportunity to connect with your loved ones. It can be an alternative to a scheduled family meal time, open up conversation around nutrition, and create a welcoming environment for sharing life updates.

Disclaimer: The nutrition information calculations are based on the nutrition database in Cronometer (www.cronometer.com), a comprehensive database with nutrition data curated from verified sources. However, it is not a guarantee of the final nutritional value based on the home cook's specific brands, ingredients, and measurements.

THE YOUNG RUNNER'S PANTRY, REFRIGERATOR, AND FREEZER

GRAINS, RICE, AND PASTA

- ❍ Dry pasta
- ❍ Soba noodles
- ❍ Old-fashioned rolled oats
- ❍ Quinoa
- ❍ White rice
- ❍ Brown rice
- ❍ Pearled couscous
- ❍ Breadcrumbs
- ❍ Nutritional yeast
- ❍ Protein powder

LEGUMES, NUTS, AND SEEDS

- ❍ Almonds
- ❍ Peanuts
- ❍ Pecans
- ❍ Walnuts
- ❍ Chia seeds

- ❍ Hemp seeds
- ❍ Pumpkin seeds
- ❍ Ground flaxseeds
- ❍ Black beans
- ❍ Cannellini beans
- ❍ Chickpeas

BAKING ESSENTIALS

- ❍ All-purpose flour
- ❍ Oat flour
- ❍ Almond flour
- ❍ Tapioca flour
- ❍ Flaxseed meal
- ❍ Baking soda
- ❍ Baking powder
- ❍ Vanilla extract
- ❍ Cacao powder
- ❍ Cacao nibs
- ❍ Chocolate chips—both semi-sweet and dark
- ❍ Honey
- ❍ Brown sugar
- ❍ White sugar
- ❍ Confectioners' sugar
- ❍ Agave syrup
- ❍ Maple syrup
- ❍ Shredded coconut
- ❍ Raisins
- ❍ Dried cranberries and blueberries

HERBS AND SPICES

- ❍ Fine sea salt
- ❍ Black peppercorns
- ❍ Chipotle chili powder
- ❍ Coriander (ground)
- ❍ Creole seasoning
- ❍ Cumin
- ❍ Garam masala
- ❍ Garlic powder
- ❍ Ginger (ground)
- ❍ Oregano
- ❍ Paprika
- ❍ Thyme
- ❍ Turmeric
- ❍ Cinnamon
- ❍ Nutmeg
- ❍ Poppyseeds
- ❍ Red pepper flakes
- ❍ Sesame seeds
- ❍ Vegetable bouillon

CANNED AND JARRED GOODS

- ❍ Spaghetti sauce
- ❍ Pizza sauce
- ❍ Chicken broth
- ❍ Vegetable broth
- ❍ Nut butters
- ❍ Mayonnaise
- ❍ Thai Kitchen® green curry paste

- ❍ Tuna
- ❍ Coconut milk
- ❍ Crushed tomatoes

OILS, SAUCES, AND VINEGARS

- ❍ Extra virgin olive oil
- ❍ Coconut oil
- ❍ Vegetable oil
- ❍ Balsamic vinegar
- ❍ Rice wine vinegar
- ❍ Apple cider vinegar
- ❍ Red wine vinegar
- ❍ Tamari sauce
- ❍ Chili garlic sauce
- ❍ Worcestershire sauce
- ❍ Dijon mustard
- ❍ Stone-ground mustard
- ❍ Frank's RedHot® sauce
- ❍ Toasted sesame oil
- ❍ Sriracha sauce

REFRIGERATOR

- ❍ Butter
- ❍ Dairy/non-dairy milk
- ❍ Eggs
- ❍ Bacon/vegetarian bacon
- ❍ Miso paste
- ❍ Tofu: silken, firm, and extra firm
- ❍ Sour cream

- ❍ Plain Greek yogurt
- ❍ Cheeses:
    - ❍ Parmesan
    - ❍ Mozzarella
    - ❍ Shredded Mexican-style
    - ❍ Cheddar
    - ❍ Feta

FREEZER

- ❍ Bananas cut into 1-inch pieces
- ❍ Blueberries
- ❍ Cherries
- ❍ Mangoes
- ❍ Pineapple
- ❍ Strawberries
- ❍ Peas
- ❍ Potato tots
- ❍ Waffles
- ❍ Plant-based ground protein
- ❍ Shelled edamame beans
- ❍ Pizza dough

PANTRY GRAB-AND-GO SNACKS

- ❍ Dried fruit
- ❍ Graham crackers
- ❍ Multi-seed crackers
- ❍ Pretzels
- ❍ Trail mix
- ❍ Jerky

REFRIGERATOR GRAB-AND-GO SNACKS

- ❍ String cheese
- ❍ Hard-boiled eggs
- ❍ Hummus with vegetables
- ❍ Yogurt
- ❍ Cottage cheese
- ❍ Fresh fruit

EQUIPMENT

- ❍ Blender
- ❍ Food processor
- ❍ Stand or hand mixer
- ❍ Parchment paper
- ❍ Butcher's twine (unbleached kitchen twine)
- ❍ Paper baking cups
- ❍ 1 tablespoon cookie scoop
- ❍ 10.5" and 12" cast-iron skillets

TIPS FOR SUCCESS IN THE KITCHEN

Cooking is a fun, creative, and most importantly, an empowering and nourishing activity. These recipes have been developed for you, the young runner, to grow and evolve into an independent, healthy athlete! Here are some tips for your success in the kitchen:

→ A successful home cook stays active in the cooking process and pays attention to their pans on the stove and in the oven. Avoid distractions and the temptation to walk away while your dish is on the stove or in the oven. You will succeed by staying engaged!

→ Create good cooking habits by reading recipes all the way through the ingredients list and the instruction steps before you begin cooking. This greatly helps to prevent surprises and ensures you are prepared.

→ Mise en place (MEEZ ahn plahs) is a widely used French cooking term that means to put in place. Essentially, it means having everything ready before beginning cooking; your oven is turned on; your pans are set out and prepared; all mixing bowls, tools, and equipment set out; all of your ingredients are measured, cut, peeled, sliced, grated, etc. before you start cooking. The recipes in this book are written under the assumption that you've prepared your mise en place and you are ready to cook.

→ Use a waste bowl when prepping meats, vegetables, and fruits. This not only keeps your work surface clean, it makes prep quicker by eliminating trips to the waste can.

→ Preparing vegetables, meat, and fish portions in similar sizes as best as possible will mean that all vegetables, meat, and fish are cooked for the same duration. This eliminates hard, crunchy, or very mushy vegetables and is especially important for meat and fish. Undercooked meat and fish contain harmful bacteria, which you should not consume.

→ Every oven is different—the best success for making sure you are not overcooking is to set a timer for the mid-way point of the total suggested cooking time. Take the opportunity to rotate your pan and adjust cooking time if you notice your item is cooking faster than the recommended total time.

- Heat your pan over the recommended heat. Test to make sure your pan is hot enough by carefully sprinkling a few droplets of water into your pan. If the water sizzles in the pan, your pan is hot enough and you can now add the oil to your pan. Waiting for the pan to reach proper temperature will create a non-stick surface to any pan.
- Every oil has a smoking point. Read the label carefully so that your oil does not smoke. If your oil smokes, that means it is burning. Not only will your food have a bitter burnt taste to it, consuming burned oil is also a carcinogen. If your oil smokes, remove the pan from the heat. Wait for it to cool a bit and carefully absorb/wipe the oil from the pan using a few pieces of wadded up paper towel. DO NOT rinse or pour the hot oil into your sink. The oil will splatter and you will experience a painful burn. Return the pan to the stove and begin again.

TIPS FOR BAKING

- Using a piece of parchment paper on your work surface when baking will make it easier to accurately measure dry ingredients. Holding your full measuring cup above the parchment, use a knife to scrape excess ingredient (such as flour) from your measuring cup onto the parchment. Then crease the paper and return the unused ingredient to its storage container.
- Use a measuring cup or a cookie scoop for portioning out batters when baking. This will ensure each portion is the

same size, and will cook for the same duration. When you have items in the same batch (think cookies or muffins) that are different amounts, some will be overcooked and others undercooked.

- If you have empty muffin tin sections and are not making a full pan, line the empty sections with a paper liner, or fill 1/2 way with water. This will prevent the empty sections from burning.

TIPS FOR PREPARING MEAT AND FISH

- Dedicate a separate cutting board to preparing raw meats and fish to avoid cross-contamination and dangerous food-borne bacteria.
- To determine if meat or fish is cooked thoroughly, purchase a meat thermometer. Insert the thermometer into the thickest part of the meat or fish. The internal cooking temperature for chicken/turkey should read 165°F; for fish 140° to 145°F.
- If you don't have a meat thermometer or are unable to purchase one, you can determine if chicken/turkey is cooked thoroughly by removing the poultry from the heat and using a knife to slice into the thickest part of the chicken/turkey. If the juices run clear, the poultry is cooked completely. If the juices have even the slightest hint of pink, more cooking is required. Thoroughly cooked meat will also slice easily—in undercooked poultry, a knife will have some resistance.
- To determine if your fish is cooked thoroughly without a meat thermometer, insert a fork into the thickest section

of the fillet and twist gently. If the fish flakes easily and has lost its translucent appearance, the fish is thoroughly cooked.

INSTRUCTIONS FOR PRESSING TOFU

1. Drain the tofu, wrap it in a paper towel, and gently press out the excess water. Remove the paper towel.
2. Fold a tea towel or more paper towels around the tofu and place it on a cutting board.
3. Set something heavy like another cutting board or a cast iron skillet on top.
4. Let the tofu rest for 30 minutes. Then, remove the tea towel or paper towels.
5. Lay the tofu on its side and slice it into three even portions.
6. Stack the portions and then slice the tofu into three even columns.
7. Rotate the tofu and slice into four rows to form squares. If you prefer smaller pieces, slice the squares diagonally to create triangles.

INSTRUCTIONS FOR ROLLING A WRAP OR A BURRITO

1. Per each recipe, scoop the recommended amount of the wrap or burrito filling and place it lengthwise, from right to left, into the center of the tortilla.
2. Shape the filling into an oblong mound the shape of a speed bump, leaving approximately 2 inches from each side of the burrito.
3. Take the back end of the burrito (the side closest to you) and fold it over the middle of the wrap, completely covering the filling.

4. Carefully roll the burrito away from you, continuing to tuck the sides and roll the tortilla wrap until all of the edges of the wrap are tucked in.
5. Place the rolled wrap, seam side down, onto a cutting board and cut with a serrated knife.

→ **For meal prep and/or freezing:** On a flat surface lay out an equal amount of sheets of aluminum foil and parchment paper. Set up the stack of sheets of foil by lining each sheet of aluminum foil with a piece of parchment paper. In the center of the parchment paper, place a tortilla, and continue by following the instructions above. Then roll the burrito in the foil and parchment for storing.

INSTRUCTIONS FOR TRUSSING (TYING) A CHICKEN

1. Lay a 3-foot length of butcher's twine on your cutting board, from left to right.
2. Pick up the chicken breast side up, with the legs toward you and place the chicken on top of the twine, so that the twine is in the center of the chicken's back.
3. Pick up the ends of the twine and pull it up just under the wings.
4. Pull the twine forward/away from you and cross it around the front of the chicken, securing the skin in place.
5. Pull the twine back toward you, across the side of the wings.
6. Bring the twine onto the breast of the chicken and cross the twine, creating an X.
7. Bring the twine underneath the ends of the legs.
8. Loop the twine around the end of each leg, and then pull the twine tightly so the legs come together.

9. Tuck the legs just under the breast and tie a double knot.
10. Trim the excess twine and continue with the recipe instructions.

INSTRUCTIONS FOR COOKING GRAINS

1. Rinse the grains in a fine sieve.
2. Heat 1 tablespoon of olive oil per 1 cup of grains in a medium saucepan over medium heat.
3. Add the uncooked grains, and stir until they are well coated. Stir constantly for about 2 minutes to lightly toast the grains.
4. The amount of liquid (water or broth) used will be twice the amount of grains, for instance, 1 cup of grains to 2 cups of liquid.
5. Pour the liquid into the saucepan and increase the heat to high. Bring to a boil.
6. Reduce the heat to low and cover the saucepan. Simmer until the grains are tender and the liquid has been absorbed, about 20 minutes.
7. Remove from the heat and let it rest for 5 minutes.
8. Fluff with a fork and serve or store in the refrigerator for up to 4 days.

BREAKFASTS

Breakfast is the fuel for champions.

—Unknown

Egg Muffin Cup with Bacon

Maple Banana Custard Oatmeal

The Best Banana Pancakes

Power Breakfast Cookie

Quinoa with Sweet Potato and Fried Eggs

Tofu Scramble

Breakfast Burritos with Tots

EGG MUFFIN CUP WITH BACON

Planning ahead to make these muffins over the weekend is not only a time saver but also ensures that you can start the day with a high-protein meal. Just two of these muffins have 30+ grams of protein. If you have extra time in the morning, consider adding sliced avocado and hot sauce. If you have access to a microwave, you could heat these for a mid-morning snack. This egg muffin is adaptable to your choice of protein and vegetables. You can substitute mushrooms or potatoes for the bacon to make it vegetarian.

1 tablespoon extra virgin olive oil

1 medium red bell pepper, chopped (about 1 cup)

1 medium onion, chopped (about 1 cup)

6 eggs, whisked

1⅓ cups almond flour

1 teaspoon fine sea salt

1 teaspoon freshly ground black pepper

2 teaspoons baking powder

8 ounces bacon, cooked and diced

⅔ cup 2% cottage cheese

1 cup shredded Mexican-style cheese, divided

Optional: avocado, hot sauce

1. Preheat the oven to 375°F. Line a 12-cup muffin pan with baking cups and set aside. If you use paper baking cups, apply a nonstick cooking spray before filling with the mixture.
2. Heat the olive oil in a medium sauté pan and add the bell peppers. Sauté the bell peppers for 1 to 2 minutes, add the onion, and cook until tender. Remove from the heat.
3. In a large bowl, whisk together the almond flour, salt, pepper, and baking powder. Add in the eggs, onions, and peppers and stir to combine. Fold in the bacon, cottage cheese, and ⅔ cup of the cheese.

4. Drop ⅓-cup portions into the muffin pan. Sprinkle the remaining cheese on the top of each muffin.
5. Bake for 20 to 25 minutes or until a toothpick inserted in the middle of a muffin comes out clean. Let cool in the pan for 5 minutes, then remove the muffins from pan.

STORAGE

→ Store the muffins in an airtight container in the refrigerator for up to 3 days.

→ **To freeze:** place the muffins in a freezer-safe zip-top bag or a freezer-safe container and freeze for up to 3 months.

TO REHEAT

Reheat in the microwave for 30 seconds. Reheat from frozen in the microwave for 90 seconds.

MAKES 12 MUFFINS

NUTRITION INFORMATION PER MUFFIN—**Calories:** 265 **Carbohydrate:** 6g **Protein:** 16g **Fat:** 20g

MAPLE BANANA CUSTARD OATMEAL

This creamy oatmeal comes together in 15 minutes, making it an easy and perfect weekday breakfast. Cooking the banana creates a thick, velvety texture and accentuates the flavor of the banana. Packed with protein and fiber, this oatmeal also provides a significant boost of manganese from the oats and pecans. Manganese is essential for bone health, metabolism, and antioxidant functions.

½ cup water
½ cup oat milk
½ teaspoon cinnamon
¼ teaspoon nutmeg
¼ teaspoon fine sea salt
2 teaspoons maple syrup
½ teaspoon vanilla extract
1 banana, sliced
½ cup old-fashioned rolled oats
2 egg whites, or ⅓ cup liquid egg whites
1 tablespoon chopped pecans
¼ cup blueberries

1. Combine the water, oat milk, cinnamon, nutmeg, salt, maple syrup, and vanilla in a medium saucepan and whisk until well mixed and the spices have been fully incorporated. Add the sliced banana and set the pan over medium-high heat. Bring to a low boil and whisk often to prevent the mixture from burning.
2. Reduce the heat to low; add the oats and whisk. Cook for 5 minutes, whisking often.
3. Slowly add the egg whites and whisk continuously for 1 minute.
4. Remove from the heat, transfer to a bowl, and top with pecans and blueberries.

STORAGE

→ You can store the oatmeal in an airtight container, separately from the toppings, in the refrigerator for up to 3 days.

TO REHEAT

→ Heat a small saucepan over medium-low heat. Add 1 to 2 tablespoons of water and the oatmeal. Stir often until thoroughly reheated. Top with pecans and blueberries.

MAKES 1⅓ CUPS OR 1 TO 2 SERVINGS

NUTRITION INFORMATION PER SERVING*—**Calories:** 503 **Carbohydrate:** 83g **Protein:** 17g **Fat:** 13g

*Based on 1 serving

THE BEST BANANA PANCAKES

These pancakes are a wholesome blend of oat and all-purpose flours, enriched with nut butter, yogurt, and ripe bananas. They're packed with fiber from oat flour and rolled oats and protein from peanut butter and eggs. The oat flour contributes iron and magnesium, and the yogurt provides calcium and probiotics for digestive health. You can substitute the peanut butter with almond butter. Enjoy them warm with a drizzle of maple syrup for a satisfying breakfast or post-workout meal. If you can't find oat flour, you can make your own by putting 1⅓ cups of old-fashioned rolled oats into a food processor or a blender and blending until you have a fine powder.

1⅓ cups oat flour
½ cup all-purpose flour
2¼ teaspoons baking powder
½ teaspoon fine sea salt
1 teaspoon cinnamon
1 teaspoon vanilla extract
⅓ cup peanut butter
1 cup 2% plain Greek yogurt
2 tablespoons maple syrup
½ cup 2% milk
2 eggs, whisked
2 small bananas, mashed
coconut oil, for frying
¼ cup old-fashioned rolled oats, for topping
maple syrup, for serving

1. Combine the oat flour, all-purpose flour, baking powder, salt, cinnamon, vanilla, nut butter, yogurt, maple syrup, milk, eggs, and banana in a large mixing bowl and stir until well combined.
2. Heat a large non-stick sauté pan over medium-low heat and add some coconut oil.
3. Drop ¼ cup portions of the batter into the pan and gently smooth out into a round shape with the back of the measuring cup.

4. Sprinkle with the dried oats and cook the pancakes until bubbles appear on the surface, and the underside looks golden brown, about 2 to 2½ minutes. Flip the pancakes and cook until golden brown.
5. Serve with maple syrup.

STORAGE

→ Store in an airtight container in the refrigerator for 4 to 5 days.

→ **To freeze:** slip a piece of parchment paper in between each pancake and placed in a freezer-safe zip-top bag, or a freezer-safe container and freeze for up to 3 months.

TO REHEAT

→ Heat the pancakes in the microwave for 10 to 20 seconds and enjoy warm.

MAKES APPROXIMATELY 14 PANCAKES

NUTRITION INFORMATION PER PANCAKE—**Calories:** 143 **Carbohydrate:** 18g **Protein:** 7g **Fat:** 5g

POWER BREAKFAST COOKIES

A cookie for a quick breakfast, a midday snack, or a post-workout boost. Old-fashioned rolled oats provide a good source of fiber, while chia seeds and ground flaxseed contribute essential omega-3 fatty acids. Dried blueberries and cranberries add antioxidants, while raw pepitas supply magnesium and iron. You can substitute almond butter with any natural, no-sugar-added nut butter.

2 cups old-fashioned rolled oats
2 teaspoons chia seeds
2 tablespoons ground flaxseed
½ teaspoon fine sea salt
½ teaspoon ground cinnamon
½ teaspoon ground ginger
⅓ cup dried blueberries
⅓ cup dried cranberries
⅓ cup raw pepitas
⅓ cup dark chocolate chips
3 tablespoons cacao nibs
1 cup natural, no-sugar-added almond butter
⅓ cup maple syrup
1 egg
vegetable oil for greasing

1. Preheat the oven to 325°F. Line two baking sheets with parchment paper and set aside.
2. Combine the oats, chia seeds, ground flaxseed, salt, cinnamon, ginger, dried blueberries and cranberries, pepitas, chocolate chips, and cacao nibs in a medium mixing bowl. Mix well and set aside.
3. Using a stand mixer or a large bowl and a hand mixer, beat together the almond butter, maple syrup, and egg until creamy and well combined.
4. Add the oat mixture to the mixing bowl, and beat well until all ingredients are evenly distributed. The dough will be very thick and sticky.

5. Lightly oil a ¼ cup measuring cup. Scoop ¼ cup-packed portions of the dough and place them on the cookie sheet, about 2 inches apart. Repeat oiling the measuring cup as needed.
6. With lightly damp hands, reshape any cookies that may have crumbled. Wet the back side of the measuring cup and gently press each cookie to flatten out slightly. Cookies should be about 1½ inches thick.
7. Bake for 16 to 18 minutes or until the edges are lightly brown. Cool on the baking sheets for 10 minutes, then transfer to a wire rack to cool completely.

STORAGE

→ Store in an airtight container at room temperature for up to 7 days.

→ **To freeze:** place the cookies in a freezer-safe zip-top bag and freeze for up to 3 months. Defrost in the morning and enjoy!

MAKES APPROXIMATELY 1 DOZEN COOKIES

NUTRITION INFORMATION PER COOKIE—**Calories:** 325 **Carbohydrate:** 33g **Protein:** 9g **Fat:** 18g

QUINOA WITH SWEET POTATO AND FRIED EGGS

This dish comes together quickly, especially if you want to make the quinoa and sweet potato in advance. The complete protein of the quinoa and the complex carbohydrate, vitamin C, and potassium of the sweet potato make a great immune-boosting recovery meal. Suggested add-ons include avocado for potassium, hemp seeds for added fiber and protein, and hot sauce for spice. You can substitute the fried egg with the Tofu Scramble on page 150 and the sweet potatoes with new potatoes.

1 cup uncooked quinoa, rinsed

1 cup water

1 cup vegetable broth

1 large sweet potato, peeled and sliced into ¼-inch thick rounds

⅛ teaspoon fine sea salt

⅛ teaspoon freshly ground black pepper

2 teaspoons extra virgin olive oil

4 eggs, fried

Optional: avocado, hot sauce, hemp seeds

1. Add the quinoa to a medium saucepan and heat over medium heat. Stir constantly for about 2 minutes to lightly toast the quinoa.
2. Add the water and broth to the saucepan and increase to high heat. Bring to a boil.
3. Reduce the heat to low and cover the saucepan. Simmer until the quinoa is tender and the liquid has been absorbed, about 15 to 20 minutes.
4. Remove from the heat and let it rest for 5 minutes.
5. Fluff the cooked quinoa with a fork and set aside.
6. While the quinoa is cooking, season the sweet potato rounds with salt and pepper.

7. Heat the oil in a medium sauté pan over medium heat. Add the potato and cover with a tight-fitting lid. Cook for about 8 minutes and flip the potatoes. Continue to cook uncovered until browned on all sides.
8. To assemble the bowls, divide the quinoa between separate bowls. Top the quinoa with the fried sweet potatoes and egg.
9. Optional: Add avocado, hot sauce, and hemp seeds.

STORAGE

→ Store in an airtight container in the refrigerator for up to 5 days.

MAKES 4 SERVINGS

NUTRITION INFORMATION PER SERVING—**Calories:** 307 **Carbohydrate:** 34g **Protein:** 13g **Fat:** 13g

TOFU SCRAMBLE

While tofu contains about 20 grams of plant-based protein per cup, it is low in methionine, one of the 9 essential amino acids (read more about the 9 essential amino acids on page 30). Nutritional yeast, however, contains all 9 essential amino acids and is rich in vitamin B, an important micronutrient for facilitating the use of amino acids. Consider substituting this scramble for the egg in the Quinoa with Sweet Potato and Fried Eggs (page 148), or the Breakfast Burritos with Tots (page 152). Or pair the scramble with toast and fruit for a simple but nutrient-dense breakfast. You can experiment with adding legumes or other vegetables, like white beans with spinach.

1 (14-ounce) block firm tofu
2 tablespoons nutritional yeast
¾ teaspoon fine sea salt
pinch of freshly ground black pepper
¼ teaspoon turmeric
¼ teaspoon garlic powder
¼ teaspoon paprika
1 tablespoon extra virgin olive oil
½ medium yellow onion, diced (about ½ cup)
½ medium red bell pepper, diced (about ½ cup)
2 tablespoons plant-based milk, like unsweetened oat or almond milk

1. Drain the tofu and place it on 2 pieces of folded paper towels on your cutting board or a plate to absorb more liquid.
2. In a small bowl, stir together the nutritional yeast, salt, black pepper, turmeric, garlic powder, and paprika. Set aside.
3. Heat the olive oil in a medium sauté pan and add the onion and bell pepper. Sauté the onion and bell pepper until just tender. Reduce the heat to low.

4. Crumble the block of tofu into the pan and continue to cook, stirring often until the water from the tofu has evaporated, about 6 minutes.
5. Add the nutritional yeast, salt, turmeric, and garlic powder. Stir to combine.
6. Pour the milk into the pan and stir quickly to combine, scraping any bits from the bottom of the pan. Immediately remove the pan from the heat.
7. Serve with toast and fruit or use as a substitute for egg in other dishes.

STORAGE

→ Store leftovers in an airtight container in the refrigerator for up to 3 days.

→ **To freeze:** place the scramble in a freezer-safe zip-top bag or a freezer-safe container and freeze for up to 3 months.

TO REHEAT

→ Place a little olive oil in a sauté pan and heat over low heat. Add the scramble and heat, stirring often until warmed through, approximately 5 to 7 minutes. Or reheat on a microwave-safe plate, covered with a paper towel on low heat for 1 to 2 minutes.

MAKES 4 SERVINGS

NUTRITION INFORMATION PER SERVING—**Calories:** 116 **Carbohydrate:** 6g **Protein:** 9g **Fat:** 7g

BREAKFAST BURRITOS WITH TOTS

Enjoy this breakfast burrito in various ways: as a quick meal tonight or follow the storage instructions for freezing and reheating for breakfast for the rest of the week. Over 20 grams of protein will sustain you until your morning snack or lunch. You can eat it on the go, or plate and serve it with avocado and hot sauce. If you are eating it as a post-run recovery meal, pair it with a smoothie or the Homemade Granola and Yogurt Bowl (page 215) for a well-rounded breakfast. To make it vegan, substitute the Tofu Scramble (page 150) for the eggs and omit the cheese or substitute with a plant-based cheese. To make it gluten free, use a gluten-free tortilla.

2½ tablespoons butter, divided

1 medium red bell pepper, chopped (about 1 cup)

½ medium onion, chopped (about ½ cup)

1 (16-ounce) package frozen potato tots

8 ounces bacon, cooked and diced

6 eggs, whisked

½ teaspoon fine sea salt

¼ teaspoon freshly ground black pepper

¾ cup shredded Mexican-style cheese

2 tablespoons chopped parsley

6 (9-inch) whole-grain tortillas

Optional: avocado, hot sauce

1. Melt 2 tablespoons butter over medium heat in a large nonstick sauté pan. Add the bell pepper and onion and sauté until just tender.
2. Add the frozen potato tots to the pan and season with salt and pepper and mix together with the bell pepper and onion. Sauté for 6 minutes, stirring every 1 to 2 minutes, moving the potatoes around so they don't stick, and then letting the tots rest in a single layer so they brown slightly.

3. Reduce heat to low and add the cooked bacon and stir together. Push the mixture to one side of the pan and melt the remaining ½ tablespoon of butter in the empty half of the sauté pan, then pour in the eggs and season the eggs with sea salt and black pepper. Scramble until the eggs are set and no longer runny.
4. Remove pan from the heat. Add the cheese and the parsley; stir to combine.
5. Heat the tortilla wraps one at a time in a clean, dry medium sized sauté pan over low heat, for 30 seconds. Flip the tortilla and heat the other side for an additional 30 seconds.
6. Remove the tortilla from the pan and continue until all tortillas have been warmed.
7. To assemble the burritos, place the filling in the middle of the wrap and roll up like a burrito. See "Instructions for Rolling a Wrap or a Burrito" on page 136.

STORAGE

→ **For meal prep:** tightly wrap each assembled tortilla in foil lined with parchment paper and store in the refrigerator for up to 5 days.

→ **To freeze:** place the wrapped burritos in a freezer-safe zip-top bag or a freezer-safe container and freeze for up to 3 months.

TO REHEAT

Remove the foil and parchment paper. Place a burrito on a microwave-safe plate and microwave on high for 1½ minutes. Turn over and microwave for another minute. Let stand for 1 minute.

Alternatively, you can thaw in the refrigerator the night before. Remove the foil and parchment paper and heat up in an oven or toaster oven at 350°F for 5 minutes.

MAKES 6 BURRITOS

NUTRITION INFORMATION PER BURRITO—**Calories:** 697 **Carbohydrate:** 55g **Protein:** 30g **Fat:** 40g

LUNCHES

Lunchtime fuel for the rest of the day's adventures.

—Unknown

CHICKEN CAESAR WRAP

This wrap is a quick and satisfying meal that combines classic Caesar salad flavors with the convenience of a handheld dish. Homemade croutons add a crispy texture, while shredded chicken and a hard-boiled egg provide a protein boost. You can use leftover chicken from the Roast Chicken with Root Vegetables (page 186) or use a store-bought rotisserie chicken. The extra croutons are great for adding to other salads.

FOR THE CROUTONS (THIS WILL MAKE EXTRA):

2 cups cubed crusty bread
3 tablespoons extra virgin olive oil
¼ teaspoon garlic powder
⅛ teaspoon fine sea salt

FOR THE WRAP:

2 cups loosely packed chopped romaine lettuce
⅓ cup cooked shredded chicken
⅓ cup halved grape tomatoes (about 6 tomatoes)
⅓ cup croutons
¼ cup grated Parmesan cheese
½ hard-boiled egg, chopped
2 tablespoons Versatile Caesar Dressing
1 (10-inch) spinach wrap

1. In a medium-size bowl, whisk together the olive oil, garlic powder, and salt.
2. Add the bread cubes and toss well. Transfer to a small sauté pan and cook over medium-low for about 10 minutes, stirring occasionally, until evenly browned. Remove the pan from the heat and let cool completely in the pan.
3. Combine the cooled croutons with the lettuce, chicken, tomatoes, Parmesan, egg, and dressing in the medium bowl and toss together.

4. Place the filling in the middle of the wrap and roll up like a burrito. See "Instructions for Rolling a Wrap or a Burrito" on page 136.

STORAGE

→ **For meal prep:** This is best served the same day so that the lettuce stays fresh, and the wrap does not get soggy. To prep the ingredients ahead of time for a quick assembly, combine the chicken, tomatoes, Parmesan cheese, and egg in a container. Place the chopped lettuce between two damp paper towels and place in a zip-top bag, seal the zip-top bag. Store the croutons and the dressing in their own separate containers. Follow steps 2 and 3 to mix and wrap.

MAKES 1 WRAP

NUTRITION INFORMATION PER SERVING—**Calories:** 561 **Carbohydrate:** 29g **Protein:** 30g **Fat:** 36g

CHICKPEA SALAD SANDWICH

This sandwich comes together so quickly as it uses common pantry and vegetable ingredients and leftover Pea Pesto Sauce (page 245). Perfect for a quick lunch or a light dinner, this sandwich is loaded with fiber and plant-based protein. Enjoy the added benefits of vitamins A and C from radishes and cucumber, and fiber and protein from chickpeas and whole wheat bread. To make it gluten free, use gluten-free bread.

1 (15-ounce) can chickpeas, rinsed and drained.

2 tablespoons lemon juice

¼ cup Pea Pesto Sauce

¼ teaspoon chipotle chili powder

¼ teaspoon fine sea salt

¼ teaspoon freshly ground black pepper

8 slices whole wheat bread

2 radishes, thinly sliced

small cucumber, thinly sliced

1. Pour the chickpeas into a food processor with the lemon juice and pulse quickly 8 to 10 times so the chickpeas still have some texture.
2. Put the chickpea mash into a medium bowl and add the pea pesto sauce, chili powder, salt, and pepper. Mix well using a fork.
3. To assemble the sandwiches, spread the chickpea mash on 4 slices of bread and top with radish and cucumber. Close the sandwiches with the remaining slices of bread. Cut the sandwiches in half and serve.

STORAGE

For meal prep: wrap the sandwiches tightly in plastic wrap or foil lined with parchment paper and store them in the refrigerator for up to 2 days.

MAKES 4 SANDWICHES

NUTRITION INFORMATION PER SANDWICH—**Calories:** 469 **Carbohydrate:** 64g **Protein:** 21g **Fat:** 16g

PEA PESTO PASTA SALAD

This bright, flavorful salad uses pea pesto sauce for a twist on traditional pesto. By adding peas, this pesto provides 16 grams of protein and a healthy dose of your daily vitamin C intake. The walnuts add essential omega-3 fatty acids, iron and B vitamins, powerful antioxidant properties, and alpha-linolenic and linoleic acids, which may have anti-inflammatory effects, making them beneficial to young runners. Add leftover roast chicken (page 186) or chicken from a store-bought rotisserie chicken to add more protein. To make vegan, omit the cheese, or sub with a plant-based cheese.

1 cup frozen peas, thawed

1½ cups halved cherry tomatoes

1½ cups quartered and sliced cucumber

1 cup mini fresh mozzarella balls, cut in half

1 teaspoon garlic powder

fine sea salt and freshly ground black pepper

4 cups dry farfalle pasta

2 cups bite-size broccoli florets

⅔ cup Pea Pesto Sauce (page 245)

1. Combine the peas, cherry tomatoes, cucumber, and mozzarella in a large mixing bowl and season with garlic powder, salt, and pepper.
2. Bring a medium saucepan of salted water to a boil. Add the pasta to the water and cook according to the package instructions.
3. Five minutes before the end of the pasta cooking time, add the broccoli florets to the saucepan. Once the pasta and broccoli are cooked, drain the pasta and broccoli, reserving about 1 cup of the starchy cooking water.

4. Return the pasta and broccoli to the saucepan and add the pesto. Stir to combine, adding some of the pasta water to thin the pesto if needed.
5. Add the pasta mixture to the large mixing bowl and toss to combine, adding more pasta water if necessary.
6. Divide the pasta salad into bowls and serve.

STORAGE

→ **For meal prep:** evenly divide the pasta salad into meal prep containers. Store in the refrigerator for up to 5 days.

MAKES 6 SERVINGS OR ABOUT 12 CUPS

NUTRITION INFORMATION PER SERVING—**Calories:** 518 **Carbohydrate:** 54g **Protein:** 20g **Fat:** 27g

QUINOA AND SWEET POTATO POWER SALAD

This fresh, bright, lemony salad provides power from protein-rich quinoa and chickpeas; beautiful color from the sweet potatoes, tomatoes and spinach; and a satisfying crunch from red cabbage, cucumber, and lettuce. By leaving the skin on the sweet potato, you'll save time and add a good source of fiber, antioxidants, and nutrients like potassium, manganese, and vitamins A, C, and E. You can substitute the chickpeas with 2 cups of leftover roast chicken (page 186) or shredded store-bought rotisserie chicken. To make it vegan, omit the cheese or substitute with plant-based cheese.

1 large sweet potato, scrubbed (leave skin on) and cut into uniform bite-sized pieces

1½ tablespoons extra virgin olive oil

fine sea salt and freshly ground black pepper

¼ teaspoon chipotle chili powder

¼ teaspoon paprika

2 cups cooked quinoa (See "Instructions for Cooking Grains" on page 138)

1 (15-ounce) can chickpeas

1 cup thinly sliced red cabbage

½ cup halved grape tomatoes

½ cup sliced and halved cucumber

⅔ cup crumbled feta cheese

2 cups packed spinach

2 cups chopped romaine

Zesty Chia Seed Dressing (page 244)

1. Preheat the oven to 425°F. Line a 9×13-inch baking sheet with parchment paper and set aside.
2. Toss the sweet potatoes with olive oil, salt, pepper, chili powder, and paprika. Spread in an even layer onto the baking sheet. Roast for 25 minutes or until the edges are browned.

3. Combine the quinoa, chickpeas, red cabbage, tomatoes, cucumber, and feta in a large bowl. (For meal prep, see special instructions below.)
4. When the sweet potatoes are finished cooking, allow them to cool before adding them to the large bowl with the other salad ingredients. Add the spinach and the romaine.
5. Drizzle with the Zesty Chia Seed Dressing and toss well to coat.
6. Divide the salad among bowls and serve immediately.

STORAGE

For meal prep:

1. Allow the ingredients to cool completely before storing.
2. Toss the sweet potatoes, quinoa, and chickpeas in a medium bowl.
3. Divide this mixture into the base of meal prep containers and top with red cabbage, tomato, cucumber, feta, spinach, and romaine.
4. Store the Zesty Chia Seed dressing in small separate containers.
5. Store in the refrigerator for up to 5 days.

MAKES 6 SERVINGS

NUTRITION INFORMATION PER SERVING (MINUS THE DRESSING)—Calories: 295 **Carbohydrate:** 41g **Protein:** 12g **Fat:** 10g

TACO BOWL WITH PLANT-BASED MEAT AND CILANTRO-LIME QUINOA

This bowl is meant to be eaten cold, making it a perfect meal prep dish for mid-week lunches. Using quinoa instead of rice boosts the protein content and adds a unique texture to this vegetarian dish. For a non-vegetarian option, ground turkey can easily replace the plant-based protein. Each serving is packed with protein, fiber, vitamins A and C, and healthy fats, making it a balanced and satisfying meal.

FOR THE CILANTRO-LIME QUINOA:

1 cup uncooked tri-color quinoa, rinsed

2 cups low-sodium vegetable broth

½ teaspoon fine sea salt (omit if using full sodium vegetable broth)

juice from one large lime, about 2 tablespoons

¼ cup chopped cilantro

FOR THE MEAT:

1 pound ground plant-based protein like Impossible or Beyond Beef, thawed if frozen

2 teaspoons extra virgin olive oil

2 teaspoons chipotle chili powder, more or less as desired

½ teaspoon ground cumin

½ teaspoon garlic powder

¼ teaspoon fine sea salt

FOR THE BEANS:

1 (15 ounce) can black beans, rinsed and drained

2 cloves garlic, minced

1 teaspoon fresh lime juice

¼ teaspoon fine sea salt

⅛ teaspoon freshly ground black pepper

FOR THE GARNISH:

¼ cup sour cream

¼ cup Frank's RedHot® Sauce, more or less as desired

2 cups quartered grape tomatoes

2 cups thinly sliced romaine lettuce

¼ cup diced carrot

2 avocados, cut into bite-sized pieces when ready to serve

1. In a medium saucepan heat the quinoa over medium heat. Stir constantly for about 2 minutes to lightly toast the quinoa.
2. Add the low-sodium vegetable broth and sea salt to the saucepan and increase the heat to high. Bring to a boil.
3. Reduce the heat to low and cover the saucepan. Simmer until the quinoa is tender and the liquid has been absorbed, about 15 to 20 minutes.
4. Remove from the heat and let it rest for 5 minutes.
5. When the quinoa is finished cooking, fluff it with a fork and transfer the quinoa to a mixing bowl. Add the lime juice and the cilantro and set aside.
6. Heat a large sauté pan on medium heat. Add the olive oil and meat. After one minute, break up the meat with a spatula and add the chili powder, ground cumin, garlic powder, and salt. Cook thoroughly, stirring often to prevent sticking, until lightly browned, about 4 to 6 minutes. Remove the pan from the heat and set aside.
7. Combine the black beans, garlic, lime juice, salt and pepper in a medium bowl. Toss to combine. Set aside.
8. In a small bowl, whisk the sour cream and hot sauce until well combined and the sauce is smooth and creamy.
9. To assemble the bowls, in the base of individual serving bowls, add the cilantro-lime quinoa, the meat, and the black beans. Top with tomatoes, lettuce, carrots and diced avocado. Drizzle with sour cream sauce and serve.

STORAGE

For meal prep:

1. Assemble the cilantro-lime quinoa, meat and black beans in the base of meal prep containers and top with tomatoes and lettuce.
2. Use small separate containers to store the sour cream sauce.
3. For the avocado, cut into quarters, leaving skin on and squeeze with lemon or lime. Tightly wrap each quarter in plastic wrap and refrigerate.
4. When ready to use, scrape away and discard the thin layer of browned avocado.
5. Store in the refrigerator for up to 5 days.

MAKES 6 SERVINGS

NUTRITION INFORMATION PER SERVING USING PLANT-BASED MEAT—**Calories:** 542 **Carbohydrate:** 53g **Protein:** 27g **Fat:** 28g

TOFU POKÉ BOWL WITH SPICY MAYO

This vegan twist on the classic poké bowl uses tofu and pearled couscous in place of fish and rice, making this a perfect next-day packable lunch. This well-rounded bowl of vegetables, protein, and fruit eats great cold and is topped with spicy mayonnaise. If you are using a reduced sodium tamari, you may want to add fine sea salt. To make it gluten free, substitute brown or white rice for the pearled couscous.

FOR THE TOFU:

1 pound extra firm tofu, drained
1 tablespoon toasted sesame oil
3 tablespoons tamari
1 tablespoon rice wine vinegar
1 clove garlic, minced
1 teaspoon minced fresh ginger
1 teaspoon white or black sesame seeds
2 tablespoons cornstarch

FOR THE COUSCOUS:

1 tablespoon extra virgin olive oil
1 cup dry pearled couscous
1 cup frozen shelled edamame beans, thawed

FOR THE SPICY MAYONNAISE:

3 tablespoons mayonnaise
3 teaspoons sriracha

FOR THE GARNISH:

2 cups thinly sliced cucumber
1 cup diced mango

1. Preheat the oven to 400°F. Line a large baking sheet with parchment paper and set aside.
2. Cut and press the tofu according to the "Instructions for Pressing Tofu" on page 136.

3. While the tofu is pressing, whisk together the sesame oil, tamari, vinegar, garlic, ginger, and sesame seeds in a medium bowl.
4. Transfer the pressed and cut tofu to this bowl and toss to combine. Drain any excess marinade and set aside to use with the couscous.
5. Sprinkle the cornstarch over the tofu and toss until evenly coated.
6. Spread the tofu onto the baking sheet in an even layer. Bake for 25 to 30 minutes, tossing the tofu halfway through, until edges are golden brown.
7. While the tofu is baking, heat the olive oil in a medium saucepan and add the couscous. Stir constantly for about 3 to 4 minutes to lightly toast the couscous. Add 2 cups of water and bring to a boil. Set the timer for 8 minutes.
8. When the timer goes off, add 1 cup of edamame to the saucepan on top of the couscous (do not stir). Set the timer for 4 mins. When the timer goes off, remove the saucepan from the heat and add the reserved marinade from the tofu. Stir to combine all the ingredients.
9. In a small bowl, whisk the mayonnaise and sriracha until well combined and the sauce is smooth and creamy.
10. To assemble the bowls, add a portion of the couscous and edamame mixture, tofu, cucumbers, and mango to each bowl. Drizzle the sriracha mayo over the top and serve.

STORAGE

For meal prep:

1. Add the couscous and edamame mixture into the base of meal prep containers and top with tofu, cucumber, and mango.
2. Store the sriracha mayo in separate small containers.
3. Store in the refrigerator for up to 5 days.

MAKES 4 SERVINGS

NUTRITION INFORMATION PER SERVING—**Calories:** 476 **Carbohydrate:** 49g **Protein:** 22g **Fat:** 23g

WAFFLE BREAKFAST SANDWICH

This breakfast sandwich, served on whole-grain waffles, strikes the perfect balance between savory and sweet, making it a delicious and protein-packed option for breakfast or lunch on the go. If you don't have a 2-quart 7×11 baking dish, you can use a square 8×8-inch baking pan. To make it gluten free, use gluten-free waffles.

6 eggs
½ cup milk
¼ teaspoon fine sea salt
⅛ teaspoon freshly ground black pepper
3 slices pork or vegetarian bacon, cooked and cut into ½-inch pieces
2 cups fresh arugula
½ cup shredded Monterey Jack cheese
1 avocado
1 cup peas, thawed
1 tablespoon extra virgin olive oil
1 tablespoon lemon juice
½ teaspoon fine sea salt
8 whole-grain waffles, lightly toasted

1. Preheat the oven to 350°F. Generously oil a 2-quart (7×11-inch) baking dish and set aside.
2. Combine the eggs, milk, salt, and pepper in a medium bowl and whisk together.
3. Pour the egg mixture into the baking dish. Fold in the bacon, arugula, and cheese until combined.
4. Bake for 15 to 20 minutes, until the eggs are set.
5. While the eggs are baking, combine the avocado, peas, olive oil, lemon juice, and salt in a food processor. Pulse the mixture 5 to 10 times until the avocado is creamy, but the peas still have some texture.
6. When the eggs are cooked, remove from the oven and allow to cool. Cut into 4 equal portions.

7. To assemble the sandwiches, spread the avocado-pea mixture on 4 waffles. Lay a portion of the eggs on top and close the sandwiches with the remaining 4 waffles.

STORAGE

- **For meal prep:** tightly wrap each sandwich in foil and store in the refrigerator for up to 4 days.
- **To freeze:** place the wrapped sandwiches in the freezer and freeze for up to 2 weeks.

TO REHEAT

- If frozen, thaw in the refrigerator overnight. Unwrap the foil and bake in an oven or toaster oven at 425°F for 8 to 10 minutes.
- Alternatively, remove the foil, place the sandwich on a microwave-safe plate and microwave on high for 1 to 2 minutes.
- The sandwiches can also be enjoyed cold.

MAKES 4 SANDWICHES

NUTRITION INFORMATION PER SANDWICH (USING PORK BACON)—Calories: 535 **Carbohydrate:** 41g **Protein:** 24g **Fat:** 32g

WHITE BEAN AND AVOCADO WRAP WITH CHIPOTLE SLAW

The combination of spicy, tangy slaw, smokey white beans, and avocado provides a vibrant, flavor-filled wrap with a satisfying crunch. Each wrap is packed with fiber and plant-based protein. The combination of healthy fats from the avocado, complex carbohydrates from the whole-grain tortillas, and antioxidants from the colorful vegetables makes them a nutritious choice that will keep you full and energized.

FOR THE QUICK-PICKLED SHALLOTS:

1 tablespoon lime juice
1 tablespoon red wine vinegar
¼ teaspoon fine sea salt
½ cup thinly sliced shallot

FOR THE CHIPOTLE SLAW:

2 tablespoons red wine vinegar
2 teaspoons lime juice
1 tablespoon extra virgin olive oil
½ teaspoon agave
1 teaspoon chipotle chili powder
¼ teaspoon fine sea salt
2 cups shredded red cabbage
1 medium carrot, shredded
¼ cup chopped fresh cilantro

FOR THE WHITE BEANS:

1 (15-ounce) can cannellini white beans, rinsed and drained
1 tablespoon extra virgin olive oil
3 tablespoons lime juice
1 clove garlic, peeled and quartered
½ teaspoon fine sea salt
¼ teaspoon paprika
¼ teaspoon chipotle chili powder
½ teaspoon cumin

FOR THE WRAPS:

4 (9-inch) whole-grain tortillas
1 avocado, quartered and sliced

1. Whisk the lime juice, vinegar, and salt in a flat-bottomed container (a meal prep container works great). Add the shallots so they are in an even layer and covered with the brine. Place in the refrigerator while you work on the slaw.
2. In a large bowl, whisk together the vinegar, lime juice, olive oil, agave, chili powder, and salt. Add the cabbage, carrot, and cilantro and mix thoroughly.
3. Remove the shallots from the refrigerator and drain and discard the brine. Add the pickled shallots to the cabbage mixture and toss until combined.
4. In a food processor, combine the beans, olive oil, lime juice, garlic, salt, paprika, chili powder, and cumin. Blend until smooth.
5. To assemble the burritos, place the filling in the middle of the wrap and roll up like a burrito. See "Instructions for Rolling a Wrap or a Burrito" on page 136.

STORAGE

→ **For meal prep:** tightly wrap each assembled tortilla in foil lined with parchment paper and store in the refrigerator for up to 5 days.

→ If you are not wrapping this up for meal prep, store the slaw and the bean mixture in separate containers in the refrigerator for up to 5 days.

MAKES 4 WRAPS

NUTRITION INFORMATION PER WRAP—**Calories:** 390 **Carboydrate:** 54g **Protein:** 13g **Fat:** 17g

DINNERS

To eat is a necessity, but to eat intelligently is an art.

—La Rochefoucauld

Chana (Chickpea) Masala

Cottage Pie

Homestyle Lasagna with Ground Turkey and Italian Sausage

Fish Burrito with Creole Seasoning

Roast Chicken with Root Vegetables

Sheet Pan Greek Turkey Meatballs and Vegetables with Lemony Rice

Spaghetti Bake

Teriyaki Salmon Bowl with Crunchy Asian Slaw

Thai Green Curry with Chicken and Sweet Potatoes

Tofu Buddha Bowl

White Bean, Potato, and Broccoli Soup

CHANA (CHICKPEA) MASALA

This stew-like chickpea masala is an excellent plant-based protein and fiber source, helping sustain energy and digestion. Tomatoes and spices are rich in antioxidants, supporting overall health, while coconut oil adds healthy fats. Serve with rice for a hearty dinner or meal prep for lunches.

4 tablespoons coconut oil

1 medium yellow onion, finely chopped (about 1 cup)

1 teaspoon fine sea salt, divided, plus more to taste

1 tablespoon ground cumin

1 tablespoon ground coriander

1 teaspoon chili powder

1 teaspoon ground turmeric

6 cloves garlic, minced

2 tablespoons minced ginger

2 tablespoons cilantro, leaves and stems finely chopped

½ teaspoon red pepper flakes

1 (28-ounce) can crushed tomatoes

2 (15-ounce) cans chickpeas, partially drained, reserving ⅓ of the liquid per can

½ cup water

1 teaspoon garam masala

2 teaspoons sugar

cooked rice (See "Instructions for Cooking Grains" on page 138)

chopped cilantro for serving

1. Heat the oil in a large saucepan over medium heat. Add the onion and ½ teaspoon of the salt and cook for 5 minutes, stirring occasionally.
2. Add the cumin, coriander, chili powder, and turmeric and stir to coat. Cook, stirring constantly, for 30 seconds.
3. Add the garlic, ginger, cilantro, and chili flakes. Cook, stirring constantly, for 30 seconds.
4. Add the crushed tomatoes, chickpeas and their reserved liquid, water, and the remaining ½ teaspoon salt. Stir, scraping the bottom of the pot to release any stuck bits of spices. At this point in cooking, the consistency will be

similar to a semi-thick soup, which will cook into more of a stew.

5. Increase heat to medium-high and cook until it reaches a gentle boil, about 2 to 3 minutes. Reduce heat to low and maintain a gentle simmer for 15 to 20 minutes or until it reaches a thick stew-like consistency, stirring occasionally.
6. Remove from the heat and stir in the garam masala and sugar.
7. Taste and adjust seasonings as needed, adding more salt for saltiness, or more sugar to offset the heat of the chili flakes.
8. To assemble the bowls, spoon the rice into the base of the individual serving bowls, and top with the chickpea masala. Garnish with chopped cilantro.

STORAGE

→ **For meal prep:** store the chickpea masala and rice in separate containers in the refrigerator for up to 7 days.

→ **To freeze:** place the chickpea masala in a freezer-safe zip-top bag or a freezer-safe container and freeze for up to 1 month. Make fresh rice when serving.

TO REHEAT

→ In a small saucepan over low heat, add 1 to 2 teaspoons of water per ⅓ cup rice. Cover the saucepan and heat the rice for 5 to 7 minutes. Place the rice in a serving bowl and add a serving of the chickpea masala to the saucepan and heat, stirring often for 7 to 9 minutes or until heated through. Serve over the heated rice.

Alternatives

If you can't find garam masala seasoning, you can make your own:

½ teaspoon dried chili flakes

½ teaspoon ground black pepper

½ teaspoon ground cumin

½ teaspoon ground cardamom

¼ teaspoon ground cloves

⅛ teaspoon ground nutmeg

MAKES 6 SERVINGS

NUTRITION INFORMATION PER SERVING—**Calories:** 360 **Carbohydrate:** 49g **Protein:** 13g **Fat:** 14g

COTTAGE PIE

This hearty dish is a nutritional powerhouse. Ground beef offers iron and zinc, while the mix of vegetables provides essential vitamins like A and C. Mushrooms add B vitamins for energy, and the Yukon gold potatoes contribute potassium for healthy blood pressure. Take note of the amount of sodium in your beef stock. If it has sodium, you may want to reduce the amount of salt added.

FOR THE VEGETABLES AND MEAT:

1 tablespoon extra virgin olive oil

1 pound ground beef

1 large onion, diced (about 1½ cups)

3 to 4 stalks celery, diced (about 1½ cups)

2 to 3 carrots, diced (about 1½ cups)

8 ounces mushrooms, halved and cut into ¼-inch slices

2 tablespoons minced garlic (about 2 large cloves)

1 tablespoon minced fresh rosemary (1 teaspoon dried)

1 tablespoon minced fresh oregano (1 teaspoon dried)

1 tablespoon minced fresh parsley (1 teaspoon dried)

1 teaspoon thyme (1/2 teaspoon dried)

2 cups 1-inch pieces fresh green beans

1 to 2 teaspoons fine sea salt

½ teaspoon freshly ground black pepper

FOR THE SLURRY:

1 cup hot water

2 tablespoons cornstarch

2 teaspoons no sodium beef stock concentrate

4 tablespoons tomato paste

2 tablespoons Worcestershire sauce

FOR THE MASHED POTATO TOPPING:

3 to 4 large Yukon gold potatoes, peeled and cubed into 2-inch pieces (about 4 cups)

½ cup milk

4 tablespoons butter

½ teaspoon garlic powder

½ teaspoon paprika

¾ teaspoon fine sea salt

¼ teaspoon freshly ground black pepper

1½ cups shredded white cheddar cheese

FOR THE GARNISH:

chopped parsley

1. Preheat the oven to 375°F.
2. Bring water to a boil in a large stock pot. Add the potatoes and simmer for 20 minutes or until fork tender. They can sit in the water until the other ingredients are ready.
3. Heat the oil in a medium cast-iron skillet over medium-high heat. Add the ground beef, breaking it up with a metal spatula or potato masher, and cook until just slightly pink. Add the onion, celery, and carrots and let cook for about 3 minutes. Then add the mushrooms, garlic, rosemary, oregano, and parsley and cook for another 3 minutes, stirring constantly. Then add the green beans and cook for an additional 3 minutes.
4. Reduce the heat to medium-low. Make the slurry by whisking together the hot water, cornstarch, beef stock concentrate, tomato paste, and Worcestershire sauce. Add it to the skillet and let the mixture simmer for 5 minutes or until the mixture is wet, but not soupy. Taste and then season with salt and pepper. If you don't have a cast iron skillet, transfer the mixture to a 9x13-inch pan.
5. Drain the potatoes and put back in the saucepan with the milk, butter, garlic powder, paprika, salt, and pepper. Mash with a potato masher until smooth and creamy.

6. Using a large spoon, dollop the potatoes over the vegetable and meat mixture and then using the back of the spoon spread them evenly over the mixture.
7. Place uncovered in the oven and bake for 15 minutes. Remove and top with the cheese. Bake for another 10 minutes until bubbling, the cheese is melted and just slightly golden.
8. Remove from the oven, sprinkle with parsley and let it sit for 10 minutes before serving.

STORAGE

→ **For meal prep:** store the cottage pie in individual meal prep containers for up to 3 days.

→ **To freeze:** place the cottage pie in a freezer-safe container and freeze for up to 2 months.

TO REHEAT

→ Place in an oven-safe dish, cover with foil and heat in a 350°F oven for 20 minutes.

→ To reheat from frozen: remove from the freezer and defrost in the refrigerator. Follow reheating instructions above.

MAKES 8 SERVINGS

NUTRITION INFORMATION PER SERVING—**Calories:** 510 **Carbohydrate:** 36g **Protein:** 30g **Fat:** 28g

HOMESTYLE LASAGNA WITH GROUND TURKEY AND ITALIAN SAUSAGE

This lasagna recipe offers a balanced mix of carbohydrates, proteins, and fats and is a perfect addition to team dinners. The tomatoes and fresh basil contribute vitamins A and C, along with antioxidants. Pair it with the Strawberry Spinach Salad with Goat Cheese (page 240) or the Caesar Salad with Toasted Walnuts (page 237).

2 tablespoons extra virgin olive oil

1 medium yellow onion, chopped (about 1 cup)

2 cloves garlic, minced

1 pound ground turkey

½ pound ground Italian sausage

1 (28-ounce) can crushed tomatoes

1 (6- ounce) can tomato paste

½ cup chopped fresh basil leaves

1½ teaspoons fine sea salt, divided

¾ teaspoon ground black pepper, divided

16 ounces ricotta cheese

1 cup grated Parmesan cheese plus ¼ cup for sprinkling

1 egg, beaten

½ pound no-boil lasagna noodles

1 pound mozzarella cheese, freshly grated (about 4 cups)

1. Preheat the oven to 400°F. Place a large sheet pan on the middle rack in the oven. Set aside a 9×13-inch baking dish.
2. Heat a large stock pot over medium-low heat and add the olive oil. Add the onion and cook for 5 minutes over medium-low heat, stirring occasionally. Add the garlic and cook, stirring, for 1 minute more.
3. Add the ground turkey and sausage, breaking it up with a fork (a potato masher actually works great for this!) and cook for 8 to 10 minutes until it is no longer pink.
4. Add the canned tomatoes, tomato paste, basil, 1 teaspoon of the salt, and ½ teaspoon of pepper. Simmer, uncovered,

for 15 to 20 minutes until slightly thickened. Remove from heat and set aside while making the ricotta mixture.

5. Place the ricotta, 1 cup of the Parmesan, the egg, and the remaining ½ teaspoon of salt and ¼ teaspoon of pepper in a medium bowl. Stir to combine and set aside.
6. Ladle 1¾ cups of the sauce into the baking dish, spreading it over the bottom of the dish. Then layer the following ingredients in this order: half of the lasagna sheets, 1¼ cups of the ricotta mixture, 2 cups of the mozzarella, and 1¾ cups of the sauce.
7. Repeat layering the ingredients one more time beginning with 1¾ cups of sauce, followed by the remainder of the lasagna sheets, 1¼ cups of the ricotta mixture, 2 cups of mozzarella. Finish with 1¾ cups of sauce. Sprinkle with the remaining ¼ cup of Parmesan.
8. Tear a piece of aluminum foil large enough to fully cover the baking dish. Spray the foil with cooking spray and cover the baking dish tightly.
9. Put in the oven on the preheated baking sheet and bake for 45 to 55 minutes or until a knife slides through the layers with little resistance.
10. Remove the lasagna from the oven and carefully remove the foil, being extra cautious of the steam being released (steam burns are very painful!). Let the lasagna rest for 15 minutes before serving.

STORAGE

→ **For meal prep:** cut the lasagna into individual portions. Store in meal prep containers in the refrigerator for up to 5 days.

→ **To freeze:** place the lasagna portions in freezer-safe containers and freeze for up to 3 months.

TO REHEAT

→ Preheat the oven to 350°F (if using a toaster oven, preheat to 325°F). Place the lasagna in an oven-safe dish and cover tightly with aluminum foil. Bake for about 30 minutes or until the lasagna is hot and the sauce is bubbling at the edges. Or reheat in a microwave, adding a few drops of water and cover with a paper towel.

MAKES 8 SERVINGS

NUTRITION INFORMATION PER SERVING—**Calories:** 719 **Carbohydrate:** 43g **Protein:** 52g **Fat:** 39g

FISH BURRITO WITH CREOLE SEASONING

This light yet hearty, flavorful fish burrito is spiced with Creole seasoning and marinated in orange juice. The orange juice not only enhances flavor but also boosts vitamin C, while the shredded cheddar cheese adds calcium for strong bones. If cod is unavailable, the recipe can be easily adapted with tilapia, pollock, or striped bass.

1 pound Pacific (True) cod
2 teaspoons Creole seasoning
1 cup orange juice
¼ cup uncooked brown rice
1 vegetable bouillon cube
1 small onion, diced
2 cloves garlic, minced
1 tablespoon extra virgin olive oil
1 avocado, peeled and sliced
1 cup shredded sharp cheddar cheese
4 (9-inch) whole-grain tortillas

1. Place the fish in a lidded sauté pan and season with Creole seasoning. Slowly pour the orange juice over the fish. Cover with the lid and let the fish marinate while the rice cooks, about 20 to 30 minutes.
2. In a small saucepan and using the bouillon, cook the rice according to the package directions.
3. Put the oil in a small sauté pan over medium heat and add the onions and garlic. Sauté until the onions are transparent and soft, about 5 to 7 minutes. Set aside.
4. When the rice is about 10 minutes from being done, heat the pan with the fish over medium heat. Bring the liquid to a low simmer. Simmer until the fish is cooked through, about 5 to 7 minutes. Cooking time may need to be adjusted depending on the thickness of your fillets. See "Tips for Preparing Meat and Fish" on page 135 for a note to determine when fish is cooked thoroughly.

5. Using a fork, flake the fish into 4 equal portions.
6. Add the onions and garlic to the rice and fluff together with a fork.
7. Heat the tortilla wraps one at a time in a clean, dry medium sized sauté pan over low heat, for 30 seconds. Flip the tortilla and heat the other side for an additional 30 seconds.
8. Remove the tortilla from the pan and continue until all tortillas have been warmed.
9. To assemble the burritos, place the rice, fish, avocado, and cheese in the middle of the wrap and roll up like a burrito. See "Instructions for Rolling a Wrap or a Burrito" on page 136.

STORAGE

→ **For meal prep:** tightly wrap each assembled tortilla in foil lined with parchment paper and store in the refrigerator for up to 5 days.

TO REHEAT

→ Remove the foil and parchment paper. Place a burrito on a microwave-safe plate and microwave on high for 1.5 minutes. Turn over and microwave for another minute. Let stand for 1 minute.

MAKES 4 SERVINGS

NUTRITION INFORMATION PER SERVING—**Calories:** 589 **Carbohydrate:** 54g **Protein:** 35g **Fat:** 26g

ROAST CHICKEN WITH ROOT VEGETABLES

This is an easy one-pan dinner in which the vegetables are coated in a rich, savory broth from the chicken. Taking the extra time to truss (tie) your chicken before roasting will achieve a beautiful roasted chicken that is tender, juicy, and uniformly cooked. See "Instructions for Trussing (Tying) a Chicken" on page 137. Each serving offers a nutritious boost with approximately 30 grams of protein. The baby red potatoes add fiber and essential nutrients, making this a balanced meal. If you have leftovers, they're perfect for transforming into the Chicken Caesar Wrap (page 156) or the Apple-Almond Chicken Salad (page 218). You can also add or substitute butternut squash or carrots.

2 medium heads fennel, tops removed and cut into wedges

1 large red onion, peeled and cut into wedges

1½ pounds baby red potatoes

1 bunch fresh thyme (about 20 sprigs), divided

1 tablespoon extra virgin olive oil

1 (4 to 5 pound) whole chicken, giblets discarded

3 teaspoons fine sea salt, divided

1 large head garlic, cut in half crossways

1 medium lemon, cut in half

2 tablespoons unsalted butter, melted

2 teaspoons freshly ground black pepper

3-foot length of butcher's twine

1. Adjust the oven rack to the lower middle position and preheat to 400°F. Set aside a 9×13 baking dish.
2. Place the fennel, onion, potatoes, and half of the thyme in a medium bowl and drizzle with the olive oil. Toss the vegetables to coat with the oil. Add the vegetables to the baking dish and spread into an even layer. Set aside.

3. Using paper towels, dry the chicken inside and out. Season the inside of the chicken with 1 teaspoon salt and stuff the cavity with the garlic, lemon, and half of the thyme. Brush the outside of the chicken with the butter and sprinkle with the rest of the salt and pepper.
4. Truss the chicken with the butcher's twine per the instructions on page 137.
5. Place the trussed chicken on top of the vegetables in the baking dish.
6. Roast the chicken for 1½ hours or until the temperature of 165°F is reached between the leg and thigh, and the thickest part of the breast. Place the chicken on a platter, cover loosely with foil and let it rest for 20 minutes. Carve the chicken and serve with the vegetables.

STORAGE

→ **For meal prep:** place the sliced cuts of chicken into meal prep containers and add a serving of the roasted vegetables. Store in the refrigerator for up to 5 days.

TO REHEAT

→ To reheat big pieces of roasted chicken still on the bone, heat the oven to 350°F, and place the chicken in a baking pan. Add ½ to 1 cup water or chicken broth to cover the bottom of the pan and cover with foil. Bake until the chicken is warmed through, 20 to 25 minutes. Remove the foil, and cook for another 5 minutes to slightly crisp the skin.

→ To reheat smaller pieces of chicken, slice your chicken into similar-sized pieces, and if possible, slice any chicken off of the bone. Place in a microwave-safe container or on a microwave-safe plate and begin with 1 to 2 minutes of reheating using the normal setting. Halfway through heating, carefully flip the chicken over so both sides heat evenly.

MAKES 6 SERVINGS

NUTRITION INFORMATION PER SERVING—**Calories:** 774 **Carbohydrate:** 35g **Protein:** 92g **Fat:** 29g

SHEET PAN GREEK TURKEY MEATBALLS AND VEGETABLES WITH LEMONY RICE

This nutritious meal combines lean turkey meatballs, rich in protein with a creamy feta yogurt sauce, which adds calcium and probiotics for digestive health. The roasted vegetables add fiber, antioxidants, and vitamins A and C, while the lemony rice offers energy-rich carbohydrates. To make it gluten free, replace the breadcrumbs with gluten-free breadcrumbs or almond flour.

FOR THE FETA YOGURT SAUCE:

½ cup plain Greek yogurt

¾ cup feta crumbles

1 tablespoon extra virgin olive oil

2 teaspoons lemon juice

1 teaspoon lemon zest

1 clove garlic

⅛ teaspoon fine sea salt

⅛ teaspoon freshly ground black pepper

water to thin the sauce as needed

FOR THE VEGETABLES:

2 cups whole cherry tomatoes

2 medium orange bell peppers, cut into ½-inch strips (about 2 cups)

1 large zucchini, cut into ½-inch half moons (about 2 cups)

1½ tablespoons extra virgin olive oil

fine sea salt and freshly ground black pepper

FOR THE MEATBALLS:

1 pound 93% lean ground turkey

1 egg

½ cup breadcrumbs

¼ red onion, finely diced (about ¼ cup)

3 cloves garlic

3 tablespoons chopped fresh parsley (or 1 tablespoon dried)

½ teaspoon dried oregano

¾ teaspoon fine sea salt

freshly ground black pepper

FOR THE LEMONY RICE:

1 tablespoon extra virgin olive oil

1 cup uncooked white basmati rice

1 cup water

1 cup chicken broth

juice from 1 lemon (about 2 tablespoons)

zest from ½ of a lemon

2 tablespoons chopped parsley

1. Preheat the oven to 400°F. Line two baking sheets with parchment paper and set aside.
2. Put the yogurt, feta, olive oil, lemon juice, lemon zest, garlic, salt, and pepper into a food processor bowl. Process until combined, but there are still some small pieces of feta for texture. Add water, 1 teaspoon at a time, as needed to reach the desired consistency for pouring over the meatballs. Store in the refrigerator until ready to use.
3. In a large bowl, toss together the tomatoes, peppers, zucchini olive oil, salt, and pepper. Place the vegetables on one of the baking sheets, and spread out evenly.
4. Put the ground turkey, egg, breadcrumbs, onion, garlic, parsley, oregano, salt, and pepper in a large bowl and mix with a fork until well combined. Use your hands to form 1½-inch meatballs and place them on the other baking sheet 2 inches apart.
5. Bake the vegetables and the meatballs for 20 minutes or until a meat thermometer reads 165°F.
6. While the meatballs and vegetables are baking, heat the olive oil in a medium saucepan over medium heat. Add the rice, and stir until it's well coated. Stir constantly for about 3 to 4 minutes to lightly toast the rice.
7. Pour in the water, chicken broth, and lemon juice and increase the heat to high. Bring to a boil.

8. Reduce the heat to low and cover the saucepan. Simmer until the rice is tender and the liquid has been absorbed, about 20 minutes.
9. Remove from the heat and let it rest for 5 minutes.
10. Add the lemon zest and parsley and fluff with a fork to mix together.
11. To assemble the bowls, add the rice to individual serving bowls, then top with the meatballs and vegetables and pour thin lines of the sauce over the top.

STORAGE

→ **For meal prep:** add the rice to the base of your meal prep containers and top with meatballs, vegetables, and sauce. Store in the refrigerator for up to 5 days.

TO REHEAT

→ Preheat the oven to 300°F and place the meatballs in a single layer on a baking sheet. Cover the baking sheet with foil. Cook for approximately 15 minutes or until heated through.

MAKES 4 TO 6 SERVINGS

NUTRITION INFORMATION PER SERVING*–Calories: 710 **Carbohydrate:** 55g **Protein:** 47g **Fat:** 34g

*based on 4 servings

SPAGHETTI BAKE

This spaghetti bake has been in our family's recipes for years. It is easily doubled for team dinners. I like to use a spicy arrabbiata sauce, but use your preferred sauce. To make it gluten free use gluten-free spaghetti. Serve with the Caesar Salad with Toasted Walnuts (see page 237) or the Strawberry Spinach Salad (page 240). The Toasted Garlic Bread (page 246) will also be a team dinner favorite.

1 egg
⅓ cup grated Parmesan cheese
1 tablespoon extra virgin olive oil
1 medium yellow onion, chopped (about 1 cup)
1 (25-ounce) jar pasta sauce
½ teaspoon Lawry's seasoned salt
12 ounces dry spaghetti
2 cups 2% cottage cheese
2 cups shredded mozzarella

1. Preheat the oven to 350°F. Set aside a 2-quart (7×11-inch) glass baking dish.
2. In a large bowl, whisk together the egg and Parmesan cheese. Set aside.
3. Bring a large stock pot of salted water to a boil. Cook the spaghetti until al dente.
4. While the pasta is cooking, heat the olive oil in a large sauté pan over medium heat. Add the onion and sauté until it is soft and translucent, about 5 minutes. Add the spaghetti sauce and seasoned salt and reduce the heat to simmer. Simmer for 15 minutes.
5. Drain the pasta and add it to the egg and Parmesan mixture and set aside.
6. Spread ¼ cup of the pasta sauce over the bottom of the glass baking dish

7. Begin layering the ingredients with ½ of the spaghetti mixture. Then spread 1 cup of the cottage cheese over the spaghetti, about 1¾ cups of the pasta sauce, and 1 cup of the mozzarella. Repeat the layers using the remainder of the spaghetti, sauce, and cheese.
8. Cover the dish with aluminum foil and cook in the oven for 40 minutes. Remove the foil and bake uncovered for another 20 minutes until the dish is bubbling and the cheese is golden.
9. Remove from the oven and let it sit for 10 minutes before serving.

STORAGE

- → **For meal prep:** cut the spaghetti bake into individual portions. Store in meal prep containers in the refrigerator for up to 5 days.
- → **To freeze:** place the spaghetti bake portions in freezer safe containers and freeze for up to 3 months.

TO REHEAT

- → Preheat the oven to 350°F (if using a toaster oven, preheat to 325°F). Place the spaghetti bake in an oven-safe dish and cover tightly with aluminum foil. Bake for about 30 minutes or until the spaghetti bake is hot and the sauce is bubbling at the edges. Or reheat in a microwave on low, adding a few drops of water and cover with a paper towel.

MAKES 8 SERVINGS

NUTRITION INFORMATION PER SERVING—**Calories:** 355 **Carbohydrate:** 45g **Protein:** 20g **Fat:** 11g

TERIYAKI SALMON BOWL WITH CRUNCHY ASIAN SLAW

This teriyaki salmon bowl is perfect for a weeknight meal. It's easy, quick, and each serving provides a nutritious boost with protein from the salmon, fiber from the vegetables, and complex carbohydrates from the brown rice. A quick homemade teriyaki sauce takes the dish to the next level.

FOR THE ASIAN SLAW:

1½ cups shredded green cabbage
1 cup shredded purple cabbage
½ cup shredded carrots
2 scallions, thinly sliced
¼ cup chopped cilantro
1 teaspoon sesame seeds

FOR THE TERIYAKI SAUCE:

¼ cup tamari
¼ cup rice wine vinegar
1 teaspoon Frank's RedHot® Sauce
1 teaspoon toasted sesame oil
I tablespoon extra virgin olive oil
3 cloves garlic, minced
2 teaspoons minced ginger
2 tablespoons brown sugar
1 tablespoon cornstarch
2 tablespoons cold water

FOR THE BOWLS:

4 6-ounce salmon filets
1 teaspoon fine sea salt
¼ teaspoon freshly ground black pepper
1 tablespoon high heat oil (like grapeseed oil)
2 cups cooked brown rice (See "Instructions for Cooking Grains" on page 138)

1. Mix the cabbages, carrots, scallions, cilantro, and sesame seeds in a medium bowl.
2. In a separate small bowl, combine the tamari, rice wine vinegar, hot sauce, sesame oil, olive oil, garlic, ginger,

and sugar. Whisk until the sugar is dissolved and the ingredients are well combined.

3. Remove ¼ cup of the teriyaki sauce and add it to the bowl with the Asian slaw ingredients. Using a fork, mix the sauce and the slaw together thoroughly, then refrigerate until ready to serve.
4. Sprinkle the salt and pepper over the fish.
5. Heat a large cast iron skillet over medium heat and add the oil. Carefully swirl the oil to coat the pan and carefully add the fillets skin side up. Don't overcrowd the pan, cook in 2 batches if necessary. Don't disturb the fillets while they cook.
6. Cook for 3 minutes, then flip the salmon skin side down using a spatula and cook for another 2 to 3 minutes. Cooking time may need to be adjusted depending on the thickness of your fillets. See "Tips for Preparing Meat and Fish" on page 135 for a note to determine when fish is cooked thoroughly.
7. When the salmon is finished cooking, remove the fillets from the skillet. The salmon should easily detach from the skin in the pan. Place on a plate while you make the teriyaki sauce.
8. Place the remaining teriyaki sauce in a small saucepan and set over medium heat. In a small bowl, combine the cornstarch and the cold water and stir until dissolved. Add the cornstarch mixture to the saucepan with the warmed sauce. Whisk constantly until well combined and the sauce thickens and coats a spoon, then remove from the heat. If it becomes too thick, add some water to thin it out.
9. To assemble the bowls, add a portion of the rice, slaw, and a fillet of salmon into each bowl. Spoon the sauce over the fillet of salmon and serve.

STORAGE

→ **For meal prep:** assemble the rice, slaw, and salmon fillet into microwave-safe meal prep containers and top with the teriyaki sauce. Store in the refrigerator for up to 3 days.

TO REHEAT

→ Place the microwave-safe meal prep container in the microwave and cover with a damp paper towel. Microwave on medium power for 1 to 2 minutes, until heated.

MAKES 4 SERVINGS

NUTRITION INFORMATION PER SERVING—**Calories:** 582 **Carbohydrate:** 43g **Protein:** 49g **Fat:** 23g

THAI GREEN COCONUT CURRY WITH CHICKEN AND SWEET POTATOES

This curry recipe combines the vibrant flavors of Thai cuisine with a balance of lean protein, sweet potatoes, and lime, which are rich in vitamins A and C for a healthy immune system. Coconut milk provides healthy fats for brain health, and the vegetables contain fiber to help maintain a healthy gut. Full-fat coconut milk is preferred, but light coconut milk can be substituted. Serve this over a bed of rice for a well-rounded meal. Substitute 1 pound of extra-firm tofu to make it vegan, following the "Instructions for Pressing Tofu" on page 136.

¼ cup coconut oil

1 pound chicken breast, cut into 1-inch pieces

1 medium yellow onion, finely diced (about 1 cup)

1 small to medium sweet potato, peeled and cut into ½-inch pieces (about 1 cup)

3 cloves garlic, minced

1 tablespoon minced fresh ginger

2 teaspoons ground coriander

1 (4-ounce) jar Thai Kitchen® brand green curry paste

1 (13.5-ounce) can full-fat coconut milk

2 tablespoons fresh lime juice

2 teaspoons sugar

1 teaspoon fine sea salt

2 cups cooked rice (See "Instructions for Cooking Grains" on page 138)

chopped cilantro for serving

1. Heat the oil in a large cast iron skillet over medium heat. Add chicken, onion, and sweet potatoes. Cook, stirring occasionally, for 6 to 7 minutes until chicken is lightly browned.

2. Add the garlic, ginger, coriander, and curry paste. Cook, stirring constantly, for 2 to 3 minutes.
3. Stir in the coconut milk, scraping the bottom of the pan to release any stuck bits. Bring to a boil, then turn the heat down to low and simmer for 10 to 12 minutes or until the chicken is done and the sweet potatoes are tender. See "Tips for Preparing Meat and Fish" on page 135 for a note to determine when chicken is cooked thoroughly.
4. Remove from the heat and stir in the lime juice, sugar, and salt.
5. Serve with rice and garnish with cilantro.

STORAGE

- **For meal prep:** add the rice to the base of your meal prep containers and top with the curry chicken and sweet potatoes. Store in the refrigerator for up to 5 days.
- **To freeze:** place the curry chicken and sweet potatoes in a freezer-safe zip-top bag or a freezer-safe container and freeze for up to 1 month. Make fresh rice when serving.

TO REHEAT

1. In a small saucepan over low heat, add 1 to 2 teaspoons of water per ⅓ cup rice.
2. Add the rice; cover the saucepan and heat the rice for 5 to 7 minutes.
3. Remove the rice from the saucepan and place in a serving bowl.

4. Add a serving of the curry chicken and sweet potatoes to the saucepan and heat, stirring often for 7 to 9 minutes or until heated through.
5. Serve over the heated rice.

MAKES 4 TO 6 SERVINGS

NUTRITION INFORMATION PER SERVING—**Calories:** 417 **Carbohydrate:** 33g **Protein:** 20g **Fat:** 23g

TOFU BUDDHA BOWL

Fuel your body with this vibrant bowl filled with plant-based protein from tofu and a creamy peanut sauce. If you want to ensure the dish is gluten free, double check that your soba noodles are made with buckwheat flour and do not have added wheat flour. This dish is ready in approximately 30 minutes, so make sure to have all your ingredients prepped before cooking.

2 cups broccoli, cut into bite-sized florets

2 tablespoons sesame oil

1 tablespoon tamari sauce

1 pound firm tofu, drained

1 (9.5-ounce) package soba noodles

2 medium carrots, finely grated

2 cups spinach leaves, washed and dried

1 tablespoon extra virgin olive oil

FOR THE PEANUT SAUCE (MAKES 2 CUPS):

¼ cup toasted sesame oil

½ cup tamari sauce

½ cup maple syrup

1 tablespoon chili garlic sauce; more or less to taste

1 tablespoon rice wine vinegar

½ cup creamy or crunchy, all-natural, no-sugar-added peanut butter

1. Preheat the oven to 400°F. Line a large baking sheet with parchment paper and set aside.
2. Put the broccoli in a small bowl and toss with the sesame oil and tamari.
3. Cut and press the tofu according to the "Instructions for Pressing Tofu" on page 136.
4. Arrange the tofu to one side of the baking sheet and spread out evenly. Distribute the broccoli on the other side of the baking sheet and spread out evenly.
5. Place in the oven and roast for 15 to 20 minutes until the tofu is golden and the broccoli is tender.

6. Put the sesame oil, tamari, maple syrup, chili garlic sauce, vinegar, and peanut butter into a blender and blend until creamy and smooth.
7. Cook the soba noodles according to package directions. When noodles are finished cooking, immediately toss them with 1 cup of the sauce and set aside.
8. Remove the tofu and broccoli from the oven and heat olive oil in a medium sauté pan over medium heat.
9. Add the tofu to the pan and toss to coat it with the olive oil. Add ⅓ cup of peanut sauce and toss to combine. Cook for about 5 minutes, stirring often. Remove from the heat.
10. To assemble the bowls, add a portion of the soba noodles into the base of each bowl. Top each bowl with a portion of the tofu, broccoli, grated carrots, and spinach leaves. Drizzle with the remaining peanut sauce.

STORAGE

→ **For meal prep:** these bowls are perfect for a next-day lunch—you don't even need to heat them up, as they are just as delicious cold. Using meal prep containers, assemble as instructed above.

→ Store in the refrigerator for up to 5 days.

MAKES 4 SERVINGS

NUTRITION INFORMATION PER SERVING–**Calories:** 740 **Carbohydrate:** 61g **Protein:** 31g **Fat:** 47g

WHITE BEAN-POTATO-BROCCOLI SOUP

This hearty vegetable soup is loaded with nutritious ingredients like Yukon gold potatoes, broccoli, and white beans. Broccoli is packed with vitamins C and K, which are essential for immune support and bone health, while white beans and vegetables contribute a healthy dose of fiber to aid digestion. It is ideal for a family dinner or meal prep. To make it vegan, omit the cheese or substitute it with a plant-based cheese.

2 tablespoons extra virgin olive oil
1 medium onion, diced (about 1 cup)
2 cloves garlic, minced
2 medium carrots, peeled and diced
1 (15-ounce) can white beans, drained and rinsed
1½ to 2 pounds Yukon gold potatoes, peeled and cut into 2-inch cubes
2 heads of broccoli, cut into 2-inch pieces, about 4 cups
1 teaspoon dried thyme
4 to 6 cups vegetable broth, enough just to cover the vegetables
1 cup grated sharp cheddar cheese
3 tablespoons apple cider vinegar
1 teaspoon fine sea salt
½ teaspoon freshly ground black pepper

1. Heat the olive oil in a large stock pot over medium heat. Add the onion, garlic and carrot and sauté until onions are translucent, about 5 to 7 minutes.
2. Add the beans, potatoes, broccoli, and thyme to the stock pot.
3. Add the broth and increase the temperature to high. Bring to a boil, cover and lower the temperature to low so that soup is simmering.
4. Simmer for about 10 minutes, until potatoes and broccoli are soft.

5. Using an immersion blender, blend until smooth. Take caution as soup may splatter. Using an oven mitt while blending the soup will protect your hand and arm. If you don't have an immersion blender, transfer soup to a blender. When using a blender with hot liquids, the heat can cause the top to blow off. For your safety, put a dish towel between the lid and the blender. This will absorb the splashing soup, and create a tight seal so the top doesn't blow off. Once smooth, return the soup to the pot.
6. Add the cheese and stir until the cheese is fully melted. Then add the apple cider vinegar, salt, and pepper. Stir the soup to combine and serve.

STORAGE

→ **For meal prep:** allow the soup to cool completely for storage. Using leak-proof containers, divide the soup into individual serving-sized portions and store in the refrigerator for up to 5 days.

→ **To freeze:** divide the soup portions into freezer-safe zip-top bags or in freezer-safe containers, leaving an extra bit of space to allow room for the liquid to expand as it freezes. Freeze for up to 2 months.

TO REHEAT

→ Thaw frozen soup in the refrigerator and reheat on the stove or in the microwave.

MAKES 5 SERVINGS OR ABOUT 10 CUPS

NUTRITION INFORMATION PER SERVING—**Calories:** 344 **Carbohydrate:** 49g **Protein:** 16g **Fat:** 11g

SMOOTHIES AND SNACKS

BERRY POWER SMOOTHIE

This nutrient-dense smoothie is rich in vitamin C, which supports immune function and tissue repair, and vitamin K, which is important for bone health. Protein from peanut butter and protein powder aids in muscle repair and growth, which is essential for recovery after intense exercise. Chia seeds contribute omega-3 fatty acids that help reduce inflammation and support heart and brain health. This smoothie is a favorite of my daughter, a collegiate runner, and provides the perfect balance of nutrients to fuel her recovery. You can use your milk and protein powder of choice.

8 ounces milk

3 tablespoons vanilla protein powder, whey or pea protein

1 teaspoon chia seeds

½ cup strawberries

½ cup blueberries

2 tablespoons peanut butter

1 banana, cut into bite-size pieces and frozen

1. Put the milk, protein powder, chia seeds, strawberries, blueberries, peanut butter, and bananas into a blender and blend until smooth and creamy.

MAKES 1 SMOOTHIE

NUTRITION INFORMATION PER SMOOTHIE*–Calories: 630 **Carbohydrate:** 88g **Protein:** 24g **Fat:** 24g

*using oat milk and vanilla pea protein powder

CHOCOLATE CHERRY RECOVERY SMOOTHIE

This protein-packed smoothie is designed to fuel your body and satisfy your chocolate cravings in a healthy way. With a blend of milk, Greek yogurt, and chocolate protein powder, it provides a rich source of protein to support muscle recovery and growth. Perfect as a post-workout recovery drink.

6 ounces milk

¼ cup nonfat vanilla Greek yogurt

3 tablespoons chocolate protein powder, whey or pea protein

1½ teaspoons cacao powder

1 tablespoon almond butter

¾ cup frozen sweet dark cherries

½ medium banana, frozen

1. Add the milk, yogurt, protein powder, cacao powder, almond butter, cherries, and banana to a blender and blend until smooth and creamy.

MAKES 1 SMOOTHIE

NUTRITION INFORMATION PER SERVING*—**Calories:** 456 **Carbohydrate:** 50g **Protein:** 33g **Fat:** 15g

*using oat milk and pea chocolate protein

MANGO AND PINEAPPLE SMOOTHIE

This smoothie can be a breakfast, snack, or post-workout recovery drink. The blend of fruits and spinach pack it with vitamins C and B6. Feel free to experiment with any nut or seed butter of choice.

12 ounces coconut water

3 tablespoons vanilla protein powder (whey or pea protein)

1 cup baby spinach

¾ cup frozen pineapple

¾ cup frozen mango

½ frozen banana

1 tablespoon nut butter of choice

Optional: ¼ to 1 teaspoon spirulina

1. Add the coconut water, protein powder, spinach, pineapple, mango, banana, nut butter, and spirulina (if using) to a blender and blend until smooth and creamy.

STORAGE

→ If you know you'll be short on time after a workout, prepare the smoothie in advance minus the liquid, then all you have to do is add the coconut water and blend.

MAKES 1 SMOOTHIE

NUTRITION INFORMATION PER SMOOTHIE*—Calories: 477 **Carbohydrate:** 68g **Protein:** 32g **Fat:** 11g

*using pea protein powder

BLUEBERRY PEACH YOGURT SMOOTHIE

Just 5 ingredients make this smoothie quick and easy to blend up. The milk and Greek yogurt provide protein and healthy fats, supporting muscle repair and keeping you full longer. The fruits add natural sugars and a boost of fiber, aiding in digestion and providing a quick energy source.

8 ounces milk
5 ounces nonfat vanilla Greek yogurt
¾ cup frozen peaches
¼ cup frozen blueberries
½ frozen banana

1. Add the milk, yogurt, peaches, blueberries, and banana to a blender and blend until smooth and creamy.

MAKES 1 SMOOTHIE

*NUTRITION INFORMATION PER SMOOTHIE**–**Calories:** 375 **Carbohydrate:** 63g **Protein:** 17g **Fat:** 8g

*using oat milk

ALMOND BUTTER BANANA BREAD WITH CHOCOLATE CHIPS AND WALNUTS

With 10 grams of protein per slice, combine this banana bread with two hard-boiled eggs, and you have a great run-out-the-door breakfast that will keep you satisfied until your mid-morning snack or lunch. Rich in calcium, iron, magnesium, and phosphorus, this yummy breakfast contributes to your body's bone development and strength.

3 medium ripe bananas, mashed
3 eggs
½ cup salted almond butter
¼ cup sugar
1 teaspoon pure vanilla extract
1½ cups almond flour
¼ cup tapioca flour
1 teaspoon baking powder
½ teaspoon baking soda
¼ teaspoon fine sea salt
½ cup semi-sweet chocolate chips
¼ cup chopped walnuts

1. Preheat the oven to 350°F. Line a 9×6-inch loaf pan with parchment paper and set aside.
2. Combine the bananas, eggs, almond butter, sugar, and vanilla in a large bowl and whisk until smooth.
3. In a medium bowl, stir together the almond flour, tapioca flour, baking powder, baking soda, and salt until combined. Add the dry mixture to the wet ingredients, mixing with a spatula until combined. Fold in the chocolate chips and walnuts. Be careful not to overmix.
4. Transfer to the loaf pan and bake in the preheated oven for 1 hour or until the loaf is golden brown and a toothpick inserted into the center comes out clean.
5. Cool completely on a wire rack before slicing.

STORAGE

→ Store in an airtight container in the refrigerator for up to 10 days.

→ **To freeze:** place the slices of bread in a freezer-safe zip-top bag and freeze for up to 3 months. Defrost the night before at room temperature.

TO REHEAT

→ Reheat slices for 10 to 15 seconds in the microwave.

MAKES 10 SLICES OF BREAD

NUTRITION INFORMATION PER SLICE—**Calories:** 342 **Carbohydrate:** 29g **Protein:** 10g **Fat:** 23g

NO-BAKE ENERGY BARS

Use this energy bar as a pre-run snack, to refuel immediately after a workout, or even as a quick bite between a run and a strength session. It's easily digestible and is rich in iron, magnesium, and phosphorus. You can substitute peanut butter for almond butter. To make it gluten free, use certified gluten-free oats.

2 cups old-fashioned rolled oats

1 cup crispy rice cereal

¼ cup ground flaxseed

¼ cup shredded coconut

½ cup dried cranberries

½ cup mini semi-sweet chocolate chips

¾ cup honey

¾ cup creamy all-natural, no-sugar-added almond butter

¼ teaspoon fine sea salt

1. Set aside a 9×13-inch baking dish.
2. Mix the oats, cereal, flaxseed, coconut, cranberries, and chocolate chips in a large bowl.
3. In a small bowl, stir the honey, almond butter, and salt until the mixture has a smooth and creamy texture. Pour over the oat mixture and use a spatula to combine, scraping the sides and bottom of the bowl to fully combine.
4. Spoon the mixture into the baking dish.
5. Put the dish into the freezer for 30 minutes to set. Once set, remove from the freezer and cut into 18 2×2-inch bars.

STORAGE

→ Store in an airtight container in the refrigerator for up to 1 week.

MAKES 18 BARS

NUTRITION INFORMATION PER BAR—**Calories:** 216 **Carbohydrate:** 28g **Protein:** 5g **Fat:** 11g

GLORIOUS MORNING MUFFINS

This wholesome, well-balanced muffin uses a variety of fruits and vegetables to create a muffin that's moist and fluffy, making it a delicious start to your morning, or any time of the day! Substitute pecans for walnuts. To make gluten free use certified gluten-free oats.

1½ cups all-purpose flour
2 teaspoons baking powder
¼ teaspoon baking soda
½ teaspoon fine sea salt
1 teaspoon ground cinnamon
¼ teaspoon ground ginger
½ cup old-fashioned rolled oats
2 cups grated carrots
1 cup peeled and grated apple
½ cup shredded coconut
½ cup chopped walnuts
½ cup raisins
2 eggs
1 medium banana, mashed
½ cup vegetable oil
⅔ cup brown sugar
¼ cup 2% plain Greek yogurt
1 teaspoon vanilla extract
1 tablespoons rolled oats, for garnish

1. Preheat the oven to 350°F. Grease or line a muffin tin with baking cups and set aside.
2. Sift together the flour, baking powder, baking soda, salt, cinnamon, and ginger in a medium bowl. Add the oats and stir to combine.
3. In the bowl of a stand mixer or a large bowl, combine the carrots, apple, coconut, walnuts, and raisins. Use a fork to stir together until evenly distributed.
4. Add the eggs, mashed banana, vegetable oil, sugar, yogurt and vanilla extract and then using the stand mixer or hand mixer, beat on low until well combined.

5. Add ¼ cup of the flour mixture and beat until smooth. Repeat this process until all of the dry ingredients are incorporated.
6. Using a ⅓ measuring cup, scoop the mixture, level off the top, and pour into the muffin tin.
7. Garnish with a few flakes of dried oats, if desired
8. Bake for 20 to 25 minutes, or until a toothpick inserted into the center comes out clean.
9. Remove the muffins from the oven and let cool for 5 minutes before transferring them to a wire rack to cool completely.

STORAGE

- Store in an airtight container at room temperature for up to 7 days.
- **To freeze:** place the muffins in a freezer-safe zip-top bag and freeze for up to 3 months. Defrost the night before at room temperature.

MAKES APPROXIMATELY 12 MUFFINS

NUTRITION INFORMATION PER MUFFIN—**Calories:** 318 **Carbohydrate:** 40g **Protein:** 6g **Fat:** 16g

HOMEMADE GRANOLA AND YOGURT BOWL

Three of the most important micronutrients for the high school runner can be found in this meal: iron, calcium, and Vitamin D. The combination of granola, Greek yogurt, and fresh berries is a mini-meal before or after a workout. This is also a great snack before bed, as Greek yogurt contains Tryptophan, which studies have shown can improve sleep by increasing melatonin in the body. Substitute another nut or nuts for the almonds or a different dried fruit for the raisins. To make gluten free use certified gluten-free oats.

FOR THE GRANOLA:

⅓ cup pure maple syrup

⅓ cup packed light brown sugar

4 teaspoons vanilla extract

½ teaspoon fine sea salt

½ cup vegetable oil

5 cups old-fashioned rolled oats

2 cups coarsely chopped raw almonds

2 cups raisins

FOR THE BOWLS:

½ cup Greek yogurt

⅓ cup granola

¼ cup fresh berries

1. Preheat the oven to 325°F. Line a large baking sheet with parchment paper and set aside.
2. In a large bowl whisk together the maple syrup, brown sugar, vanilla, and salt. Then, whisk in the oil. Gently fold in the oats and almonds until coated in the maple syrup mixture.
3. Spread the oat and almond mixture in a thin, even layer across the baking sheet. Using a spatula, press the mixture to make it compact.

4. Bake until lightly browned, 40 to 45 minutes, rotating the pan once halfway through baking. Remove from the oven and cool the granola on a wire rack for at least 45 minutes.
5. Break the cooled granola into pieces of desired size. Stir in the raisins.
6. To assemble the bowl, first layer the yogurt, then granola, and finally the berries.

STORAGE

→ Store the granola in an airtight container at room temperature for up to 2 weeks.

MAKES 6 CUPS GRANOLA AND 1 SERVING YOGURT BOWL

NUTRITION INFORMATION PER BOWL—**Calories:** 439 **Carbohydrate:** 59g **Protein:** 18g **Fat:** 16g

QUICK AND EASY

"Every time you eat is an opportunity to nourish your body."

— Unknown

Apple-Almond Chicken Salad

Peanut Butter and Jam Overnight Oats

Pea Pesto Grilled Cheese

Sardine Toast

Nutella Mousse Parfait

Tuna Salad with Green Goddess Dressing

Weeknight Cast Iron Skillet Pizza

APPLE-ALMOND CHICKEN SALAD

This chicken salad provides a good mix of protein, healthy fats, and fiber. The shredded chicken offers lean protein, essential for muscle repair and maintenance. The apples and celery contribute dietary fiber, supporting digestion. Chopped almonds supply healthy fats, while the Greek yogurt adds probiotics, which are beneficial for gut health. You can use leftover chicken from the Roast Chicken with Root Vegetables (page 186) or a store-bought rotisserie chicken for ease on a busy day.

3 cups cooked shredded chicken

1 medium apple cut into small cubes (about ¾ cup)

½ cup golden raisins

2 stalks celery, chopped (about ½ cup)

½ cup chopped almonds

3 green onions, white and light green parts only, chopped (about ¼ cup)

½ cup mayonnaise

⅓ cup plain Greek yogurt

3 tablespoons Dijon mustard

1 teaspoon apple cider vinegar

¼ teaspoon fine sea salt

⅛ teaspoon freshly ground black pepper

1. Place the chicken, apple, raisins, celery, almonds, green onions, mayonnaise, yogurt, mustard, vinegar, salt, and pepper in a large bowl. Stir until well combined.
2. Serve alongside crackers, cheese, and vegetable sticks or as a sandwich on whole-grain bread with fresh lettuce.

STORAGE

→ **For meal prep:** divide chicken salad into individual airtight containers and store in the refrigerator for up to 4 days. Store accompaniments separately.

MAKES 4 SERVINGS

NUTRITION INFORMATION PER SERVING—**Calories:** 569 **Carbohydrate:** 27g **Protein:** 40g **Fat:** 34g

PEANUT BUTTER AND JAM OVERNIGHT OATS

Overnight oats are a versatile meal prep option that makes mornings easier. Packed with fiber, protein, and healthy fats, this recipe is perfect for a quick breakfast or a satisfying snack any time of day. Customize it with your favorite nut butter, jam, and berries. To make it gluten free, use certified gluten free oats.

2 cups old-fashioned rolled oats
2 cups milk
1 cup 2% plain Greek yogurt
2 teaspoons maple syrup
4 tablespoons natural, no-added-sugar peanut butter (creamy or crunchy)
4 tablespoons jam
4 teaspoons chia seeds
1 cup berries

1. Put all of the ingredients except for the berries into a large bowl and stir until just combined.
2. Divide into 4 containers with tightly fitting lids and refrigerate overnight.
3. When ready to serve, stir, and then top with the fresh berries

STORAGE

→ Overnight oats will keep in the refrigerator for up to 4 days.

MAKES 4 SERVINGS

NUTRITION INFORMATION PER SERVING—**Calories:** 451 **Carbohydrate:** 65g **Protein:** 17g **Fat:** 14g

PEA PESTO GRILLED CHEESE

This elevated grilled cheese is quick, easy, and satisfying, making it a great post-Saturday-practice lunch or dinner. To make it gluten free, use gluten-free bread.

2 teaspoons butter, softened

2 pieces whole-grain bread

2 tablespoons Pea Pesto Sauce (page 245)

2 slices cheddar cheese

1 tablespoons butter

1. Place the bread on a cutting board and spread a thin layer of butter on one side of both pieces of the bread. Flip the bread pieces over and spread 1 tablespoon of the Pea Pesto Sauce on each piece of bread.
2. Layer the cheese on top of the pesto and close to make a sandwich, butter side out.
3. Heat a nonstick or cast-iron skillet over medium-low heat and melt enough butter to coat the bottom of the skillet
4. Place the sandwich in the skillet and cover with a lid and cook for 3 to 4 minutes until the bottom slice is golden brown and crispy.
5. Flip the sandwich, cover the skillet again, and cook until this side is also golden brown and crispy, about 2 to 3 minutes. Reduce the heat to low if the bread is browning too much before the cheese is melted.
6. Remove from the skillet and let it rest on the cutting board for 3 to 5 minutes before slicing.

MAKES 1 SANDWICH

NUTRITION INFORMATION PER SANDWICH—**Calories:** 689 **Carbohydrate:** 32g **Protein:** 17g **Fat:** 56g

SARDINE TOAST

Sardines are packed with omega-3 fatty acids, calcium, and vitamin D—excellent for heart and bone health. A fried egg adds extra protein and richness, making it a satisfying option for any time of day. Serve it with a simple green salad to round it out as a dinner.

1 slice sourdough bread, sliced approximately ½- to ¾-inch thick and toasted

1 tablespoon herbed goat cheese

¼ teaspoon fresh lemon juice

¼ teaspoon balsamic vinegar

½ (4-ounce) can sardines, preferably canned in extra virgin olive oil

1 radish, thinly sliced

¼ cup spring mix greens

1 teaspoon butter

1 egg

fine sea salt and freshly ground black pepper

1. Spread the goat cheese on the toast and drizzle with lemon juice and balsamic vinegar.
2. Carefully lay the sardines on top of the goat cheese and top with radish slices and the greens.
3. Heat butter in a small sauté pan and add the egg. Let the egg cook until the white is set and the yolk is done to your liking.
4. Season with salt and pepper.

STORAGE

→ Transfer the remaining sardines to an airtight container and store them in the refrigerator for up to 3 days.

MAKES 1 SERVING

NUTRITION INFORMATION PER SERVING—**Calories:** 451 **Carbohydrate:** 24g **Protein:** 22g **Fat:** 31g

NUTELLA MOUSSE PARFAIT

You will be amazed at how quick and easy this Nutella Mousse Parfait is to make. Creamy and decadent, but also healthy and rich in protein. Get fancy and have fun with your presentation by using a parfait glass or a delicate crystal bowl! To make it vegan, use a vegan whipped cream.

1 (14-ounce) package silken tofu, drained

⅔ cup Nutella

2 cups store-bought whipped cream

4 teaspoons chopped peanuts

dark chocolate for shaving

1. Blend the tofu and the Nutella in a food processor until smooth, scraping down the sides as necessary.
2. Put the mousse in a measuring cup with a spout and then pour ½ cup portions into 4 glasses.
3. Cover each glass with plastic wrap and place in the refrigerator until set, at least 30 minutes.
4. Top with whipped cream and peanuts.
5. Using a vegetable peeler, carefully shave the chocolate directly over your parfait.

STORAGE

→ Store the mousse in individual containers in the refrigerator for up to 5 days. Add toppings when ready to serve.

MAKES 4 SERVINGS

NUTRITION INFORMATION PER SERVING—**Calories:** 427 **Carbohydrate:** 39g **Protein:** 11g **Fat:** 25g

TUNA SALAD WITH GREEN GODDESS DRESSING

Green Goddess Dressing elevates canned tuna to a new experience and makes this a convenient, herbaceous lunch when you might be short on time.

1 (5-ounce) can tuna, drained

⅓ cup Green Goddess Dressing (page 243)

fine sea salt and freshly ground black pepper

pita, pretzel, or tortilla chips for serving

1. Put the tuna in a medium bowl and gently separate the tuna with a fork.
2. Pour the dressing over the tuna and stir to combine. Taste and adjust salt and pepper as needed, keeping in mind that the chip you use could be salty enough.

MAKES 1 SERVING

NUTRITION INFORMATION PER SERVING (MINUS THE CHIPS)—Calories: 215
Carbohydrate: 5g **Protein:** 36g **Fat:** 5g

WEEKNIGHT CAST IRON SKILLET PIZZA

This pizza conveniently uses one pan that creates a deep dish pizza with a crispy bottom and an ooey-gooey cheese topping. It's also completely adaptable to your tastes and what you have on hand, making the perfect weeknight meal. Serve with the Caesar Salad with Toasted Walnuts on page 237. To make it gluten free, use gluten-free pizza dough. For a vegan option, substitute a plant-based cheese.

1 tablespoon extra virgin olive oil
¼ cup sliced onion
1 cup sliced mushrooms
all-purpose flour for dusting
16 ounces frozen pizza dough, thawed
⅓ cup pizza sauce
1 cup grated mozzarella cheese

1. Preheat the oven to 500°F.
2. Heat a 10.5-inch cast iron skillet (or other oven-safe skillet) over medium heat and pour in the olive oil.
3. Add the onion and mushrooms to the skillet and sauté, stirring occasionally. Cook until the onions are transparent, and the mushrooms are tender and their juices have cooked away, about 8 to 10 minutes.
4. Turn the heat off, remove the mushrooms and onion from the skillet into a small bowl and set aside. Return the skillet to the warm burner. Add more olive oil to coat the pan if necessary.
5. Dust a work surface with the flour and stretch or roll the dough to approximately 10.5 inches in diameter using either your hands or a rolling pin.

6. Carefully, using caution not to touch the sides of the skillet, place the dough into the skillet and stretch the dough to cover the base.
7. Spoon and spread the pizza sauce to cover the dough, then add the mushrooms and onions. Top with cheese.
8. Carefully place the hot skillet into the oven and cook for 9 to 11 minutes, until the cheese is bubbly and the dough is slightly browning along the edges.
9. Remove the skillet from the oven. Remove the pizza from the skillet and place on a cutting board. Allow to rest for 5 minutes before slicing into 6 even slices.

STORAGE

→ This pizza is delicious the next day for lunch—eaten cold or warm! Store leftovers in an airtight container in the refrigerator for 3 to 4 days.

TO REHEAT

→ **Preheat the oven to 350°F.** Place the pizza slices on a large piece of foil and place it directly on the center rack of the oven. Bake for 8 to 10 minutes until the cheese is melted and the bottoms are golden and crisp. If using a toaster oven, bake for 3 to 4 minutes.

MAKES 1 6-SLICE PIZZA OR ABOUT 2 TO 3 SERVINGS

NUTRITION INFORMATION PER 2-PIECE SERVING—**Calories:** 524 **Carbohydrate:** 73g **Protein:** 24g **Fat:** 15g

DESSERTS

A party without cake is just a meeting.

— Julia Child

CARROT CUPCAKE WITH CREAM CHEESE FROSTING

This recipe makes a fluffy, moist, and carroty cupcake with a light cream cheese frosting for your next celebration or gathering.

1¾ cups all-purpose flour
½ cup almond flour
2 teaspoons baking soda
1 teaspoon fine sea salt
1½ teaspoons cinnamon
1 teaspoon ground ginger
½ cup dark brown sugar
¾ cup extra virgin olive oil
3 eggs
1 teaspoon vanilla extract
2 cups grated carrots

FOR THE CREAM CHEESE FROSTING:

1 (8-ounce) package cream cheese at room temperature
1½ cups confectioners' sugar, sifted
2 teaspoons vanilla extract
1teaspoon lemon zest

1. Preheat the oven to 350°F. Line the muffin pan with baking cups and set aside.
2. Sift together the all-purpose flour, almond flour, baking soda, salt, cinnamon and ginger in a large bowl and set aside.
3. In the bowl of a stand mixer or a large bowl, mix the brown sugar, oil, eggs and vanilla. Using the stand mixer or hand mixer, beat until well combined.
4. Add the dry ingredients and beat until all ingredients are thoroughly combined. Add the carrots and mix together on the lowest setting of your mixer.
5. Using a ⅓-cup measure, fill the baking cups with the batter. Bake for 18 to 20 minutes, or until a toothpick stuck in the center of the muffin comes out clean.

6. In the bowl of a stand mixer or a large bowl, beat together the cream cheese, confectioners' sugar, vanilla extract, and lemon zest until smooth and creamy. Place the frosting in a bowl, cover and store in the refrigerator until ready to use.
7. Let cupcakes rest in the muffin tin for 10 minutes, then transfer to a wire rack to cool completely before frosting.
8. Remove the frosting from the refrigerator and using a butter knife, spread the frosting over each cupcake. For best results, frost cupcakes right before serving.

STORAGE

→ Store the cupcakes in an airtight container at room temperature for up to 4 days. Store the frosting in the refrigerator for up to 7 days.

MAKES 12 LARGE CUPCAKES AND 1 CUP FROSTING

NUTRITION INFORMATION PER CUPCAKE WITH FROSTING—**Calories:** 401 **Carbohydrate:** 42g **Protein:** 6g **Fat:** 24g

FUDGY CHOCOLATE CHIA PUDDING

This healthy, satisfying dessert is thick, creamy, and fudgy, making it perfect for meal prep. It is packed with protein from chia seeds and nut butter, fiber from bananas and chia seeds, and healthy fats from coconut milk and nut butter. Feel free to substitute with any all-natural, no-sugar-added nut butter.

2 medium ripe bananas

⅓ cup raw cacao powder

½ cup chia seeds

½ cup all-natural, no-sugar-added peanut butter

2 tablespoons maple syrup

1 (13.5-ounce) can full-fat coconut milk

½ teaspoon pure vanilla extract

pinch of fine sea salt

berries of your choice, for garnish

2½ tablespoons of chopped peanuts, for garnish, optional

1. In a medium bowl, mash the bananas with a fork until smooth. Sift the cacao powder into the bowl with the bananas, and then add the chia seeds, peanut butter, maple syrup, coconut milk, vanilla extract, and salt. Whisk together.
2. Pour ½ cup servings into 8 individual jars. Place the jars in the refrigerator for 3 to 5 hours or overnight.
3. Garnish with the berries of your choice and 1 teaspoon of chopped peanuts, if using.

STORAGE

→ Store tightly wrapped in the refrigerator for 5 to 7 days.

MAKES 8 SERVINGS

NUTRITION INFORMATION PER SERVING*–**Calories:** 308 **Carbohydrate:** 22g **Protein:** 9g **Fat:** 22g

*without berries or peanuts

JAM DOT COOKIE

These jammy-nutty cookies are made with coconut oil, pure maple syrup, and almond flour, making them gluten free and vegan. They provide healthy fats and natural sweetness and are a good source of protein and fiber. Adding fruit jam adds a burst of flavor, creating a delicious treat suitable for various dietary preferences.

2½ cups almond flour
¼ teaspoon baking soda
¼ teaspoon fine sea salt
⅓ cup coconut oil, melted
¼ cup pure maple syrup
1 teaspoon vanilla extract
2 tablespoons all-fruit jam

1. Sift together the almond flour, baking soda, and salt in a medium bowl.
2. Using a stand mixer or a large bowl and a hand mixer, beat together the coconut oil, maple syrup, and vanilla.
3. Add the dry ingredients to the wet ingredients and mix until a dough forms.
4. Cover the dough and place in the refrigerator to chill for one hour or up to two days.
5. Preheat the oven to 350°F and line a baking sheet with parchment paper.
6. Using a tablespoon to scoop out the dough, gently roll the dough into balls and place on the baking sheet about 2 inches apart.
7. Use the back of a ¼ teaspoon to make an indentation in the center of each ball.
8. Fill each indentation with a ¼ teaspoon of jam.

9. Bake for 10 to 12 minutes or until the edges of the cookies are golden brown. Cool on the baking sheets for 5 minutes, then transfer the cookies to a wire rack to cool completely.

STORAGE

→ Store cookies in an airtight container at room temperature for 5 days.

TO REHEAT

→ These cookies are best served within an hour of baking since almond flour cookies tend to soften as they sit at room temperature—but they are still delicious when they are soft! A simple trick to re-crisp almond flour cookies is to reheat them on a parchment-lined baking sheet in a 195°F oven for about 6 to10 minutes.

MAKES 12 TO 15 COOKIES

NUTRITION INFORMATION PER COOKIE –**Calories:** 215 **Carbohydrate:** 11g **Protein:** 5g **Fat:** 18g

*based on 12 cookies

THE ULTIMATE OATMEAL RAISIN COOKIE

This cookie features oat flour and rolled oats for a hearty texture, with ground flaxseed adding a boost of fiber and omega-3 fatty acids. It combines the flavors of three of the most classic cookies—peanut butter, chocolate chips, and raisins—to create one fantastic cookie. It's also gluten free and vegan.

1 tablespoon ground flaxseed

3 tablespoons very hot water

¾ cup oat flour

1½ cups old-fashioned rolled oats

¼ teaspoon baking soda

1 teaspoon baking powder

½ teaspoon fine sea salt

½ teaspoon cinnamon

½ cup vegetable shortening

½ cup packed brown sugar

¼ cup maple syrup

1 cup all-natural, no-sugar-added peanut butter

1 teaspoon vanilla extract

1 cup raisins

¾ cup dark chocolate chips

Optional: 1 teaspoon flaky sea salt for sprinkling

1. Preheat the oven to 375 °F. Line 2 baking sheets with parchment paper and set aside.
2. Combine the ground flax seed and hot water in a small bowl. Stir together with a fork and set aside for at least 5 minutes (longer is OK), while working on the next steps.
3. Sift the oat flour into a medium bowl, then add the oats, baking soda, baking powder, salt and cinnamon. Stir to combine and set aside.
4. Using a stand mixer or a large bowl and a hand mixer, beat the vegetable shortening and the brown sugar until creamy and well combined. Small visible pieces of shortening are okay. Add the maple syrup and peanut butter, and beat to combine. Scrape down the sides of the bowl and add the flaxseed mixture and the vanilla and beat until combined.

5. Add the oat mixture to the mixing bowl, and mix well.
6. On the lowest mixer setting, add the raisins and the chocolate chips and mix well.
7. Using a 1 tablespoon cookie scoop, scoop out the dough and place on the baking sheets, about 2 inches apart.
8. Dampen the bottom of a small glass and gently press the cookies to flatten slightly. If using, lightly sprinkle the tops of the cookies with the sea salt.
9. Bake for 10 to 12 minutes, until the edges of the cookies are golden brown but the centers are still soft. Cool on the baking sheets for 5 to 6 minutes, then transfer the cookies to a wire rack to cool completely.

STORAGE

→ Store at room temperature in an airtight container for up to 7 days.

→ **To freeze:** place the cookies in a freezer-safe zip-top bag and freeze for up to 3 months. Defrost at room temperature.

MAKES ABOUT 3 DOZEN COOKIES

NUTRITION INFORMATION PER COOKIE–**Calories:** 150 **Carbohydrate:** 18g **Protein:** 3g **Fat:** 8g

SIDES, SAUCES, AND DRESSINGS

CAESAR SALAD WITH TOASTED WALNUTS

Kale is rich in vitamins A, C, and K, as well as antioxidants and fiber. Romaine provides a crisp bite along with vitamins A and K. Walnuts add healthy fats and protein, while Parmesan contributes calcium. This pairs as a side with the Spaghetti Bake (page 192) and can easily be doubled or tripled for team dinners.

¾ cup halved walnuts

1 bunch of curly kale, chopped into bite sized pieces (about 2 cups)

1 bunch of romaine, chopped into bite sized pieces (about 3 cups)

½ cup shredded Parmesan

½ cup Versatile Caesar Dressing (page 239)

1. In a small skillet over medium to low heat lightly toast the walnut pieces approximately 4 minutes. Gently tossing so they do not burn.
2. Combine the kale, romaine, walnuts, and Parmesan in a large serving bowl.
3. If serving immediately, toss with the Versatile Caesar Dressing.

STORAGE

→ **For meal prep:** place the undressed greens, walnuts and Parmesan in meal prep containers. Store the Versatile Caesar Dressing in small separate containers. Salad can be stored in the refrigerator for up to 2 days.

MAKES 4 TO 6 SERVINGS

NUTRITION INFORMATION PER SERVING*—**Calories:** 334 **Carbohydrate:** 6g **Protein:** 8g **Fat:** 32g

*based on 4 servings

VERSATILE CAESAR DRESSING

This Caesar Dressing can be used for the Caesar Salad with Toasted Walnuts (page 237), Chicken Caesar Wrap (page 156), in place of mayo for tuna or chicken salad, or for dipping with your favorite vegetables.

1 cup mayonnaise

¼ cup lemon juice

2 tablespoons miso paste

2 small cloves garlic, roughly chopped

1 tablespoon apple cider vinegar

1½ teaspoons Dijon mustard

1 teaspoon freshly ground black pepper

½ cup extra virgin olive oil

1. Place mayonnaise, lemon juice, miso paste, garlic, vinegar, mustard, and pepper in a blender and blend until combined.
2. With the blender running, slowly add the olive oil to emulsify.

STORAGE

→ Store in a jar with a tightly fitting lid in the refrigerator for up to 10 days. Give it a good shake before use.

MAKES 2 CUPS

NUTRITION INFORMATION PER 1/2 CUP SERVING—**Calories:** 639 **Carbohydrate:** 5g **Protein:** 2g, **Fat:** 69g

STRAWBERRY SPINACH SALAD WITH GOAT CHEESE

Baby spinach provides a rich source of vitamins A, C, and K, along with iron and antioxidants. Strawberries add a burst of natural sweetness and are high in vitamin C and manganese. Creamy goat cheese offers protein and calcium, while toasted slivered almonds bring healthy fats, protein, and a satisfying crunch. The Creamy Poppyseed Dressing (page 242) ties everything together with a sweet and tangy flavor.

½ cup slivered almonds, toasted
5 cups baby spinach
1¾ cups halved and thinly sliced strawberries
5 ounces goat cheese crumbles
½ cup Creamy Poppyseed Dressing

1. In a small skillet over medium to low heat lightly toast the slivered almonds for approximately 4 minutes. Gently tossing so they do not burn.
2. Combine the spinach, strawberries and goat cheese in a large serving bowl.
3. If serving immediately, toss with the Cream Poppyseed Dressing.

STORAGE

→ **For meal prep:** place the undressed greens, almonds and goat cheese in meal prep containers. Store the Creamy Poppyseed Dressing in small separate containers. Salad can be stored in the refrigerator for up to 2 days.

MAKES 4 TO 6 SERVINGS

NUTRITION INFORMATION PER SERVING*–**Calories:** 322 **Carbohydrate:** 13g **Protein:** 13g **Fat:** 25g

*based on 4 servings

CREAMY POPPYSEED DRESSING

This creamy poppyseed dressing is quick and easy—coming together in less than 10 minutes—it will make you realize how simple and cost effective, not to mention how fresh and tasty it is to make your own dressings. This recipe makes the perfect amount to go with the Strawberry Spinach Salad with Goat Cheese (page 240), but can also be easily doubled.

- ¼ cup 2% plain Greek yogurt
- 2 teaspoons mayonnaise
- 2 tablespoons extra virgin olive oil
- 1 tablespoon apple cider vinegar
- 2 teaspoons honey
- 2 teaspoons poppyseeds
- ½ teaspoon fine sea salt

1. In a medium bowl, whisk the yogurt, mayonnaise, olive oil, vinegar, honey, poppyseeds, and salt until well combined and the dressing is smooth and creamy.

STORAGE

→ Store dressing in a jar with a tightly fitting lid in the refrigerator for up to 5 days. Give it a good shake before use.

MAKES ½ CUP

NUTRITION INFORMATION PER SERVING–**Calories:** 421 **Carbohydrate:** 15g **Protein:** 7g **Fat:** 38g

GREEN GODDESS DRESSING

This vibrant, tangy dressing is made with fresh spring herbs and Greek yogurt and comes together quickly. It brightens up Tuna Salad with Green Goddess Dressing (page 225).

- 1 cup tightly packed parsley (delicate stems okay)
- ⅓ cup tightly packed basil leaves
- ¼ cup snipped chives
- 1 small clove garlic, quartered
- ¾ teaspoon lemon zest
- ½ cup lemon juice
- 1 teaspoon agave
- 1 cup 2% plain Greek yogurt
- ½ teaspoon fine sea salt
- ¼ teaspoon freshly ground black pepper

1. Put the parsley, basil, chives, garlic, lemon zest, lemon juice, agave, yogurt, salt, and pepper into a food processor, and process until smooth with flecks of green herbs remaining.
2. Taste and adjust the salt and pepper, if needed.

STORAGE

→ Store in a jar with a tightly fitting lid in the refrigerator for 5 to 7 days. Give it a good shake before use.

MAKES 1¾ CUPS

NUTRITION INFORMATION PER SERVING—**Calories:** 246 **Carbohydrate:** 24g **Protein:** 27g **Fat:** 6g

ZESTY CHIA SEED DRESSING

This light and zesty lemon-chia seed dressing is a perfect blend of tangy and sweet. The chia seeds not only add a slight crunch but also boost the nutritional value, and it pairs perfectly with the Quinoa and Sweet Potato Power Salad (page 162) or drizzled over roasted vegetables.

¼ cup extra virgin olive oil
½ teaspoon lemon zest
2 tablespoons fresh lemon juice
2 tablespoons apple cider vinegar
1 teaspoon stone ground mustard
2 teaspoons agave
2 teaspoons chia seeds
fine sea salt and freshly ground black pepper

1. Combine the olive oil, lemon zest, lemon juice, apple cider vinegar, mustard, agave, and chia seeds in a small jar with a tightly fitting lid.
2. Close the jar tightly and shake the dressing until well combined. Season with salt and pepper to taste. Shake again.

STORAGE

→ Store in the refrigerator for up to 2 weeks. Give it a good shake before use.

MAKES ½ CUP (8 1-TABLESPOON SERVINGS)

NUTRITION INFORMATION PER SERVING—**Calories:** 71 **Carbohydrate:** 2g **Protein:** 0g **Fat:** 7g

PEA PESTO SAUCE

This bright, flavorful pesto is packed with healthy fats from walnuts and olive oil, protein from Parmesan cheese and peas, and vitamins from fresh basil and peas. Enjoy it in the Pea Pesto Pasta Salad, Chickpea Salad Sandwich, and the Pea Pesto Grilled Cheese.

1 cup basil, packed
1 clove garlic
½ cup walnuts
⅓ cup grated Parmesan
¾ cup frozen peas, thawed
⅓ cup extra virgin olive oil
2 teaspoons lemon juice
fine sea salt and freshly ground black pepper

1. Put the basil, garlic, walnuts, Parmesan cheese, peas, olive oil, lemon juice, salt and pepper into a food processor and blend until smooth.

STORAGE

→ Store pesto in an airtight container, with the top layer covered in olive oil to prevent browning, for up to 7 days.

→ **To freeze:** place pesto in a freezer-safe zip-top bag or in a freezer-safe container, leaving an extra bit of space to allow room for the liquid to expand as it freezes. Freeze for up to 3 months.

MAKES 1 CUP

NUTRITION INFORMATION PER SERVING—**Calories:** 1195 **Carbohydrate:** 28g **Protein:** 23g **Fat:** 114g

TOASTED GARLIC BREAD

Make this crunchy, savory, restaurant-style garlic bread to go with the Spaghetti Bake (page 192) for a weeknight dinner, or for your contribution to the next team dinner. If using unsalted butter, sprinkle bread halves with ½ teaspoon fine sea salt just before bread goes in the oven.

6 cloves garlic, chopped finely
1 stick salted butter
1 tablespoon chopped parsley
1 tablespoon grated Parmesan cheese
French baguette

1. Preheat the oven to 350°F. Set aside 2 medium baking sheets.
2. Set a small saucepan over low heat and add the butter to melt, keeping an eye on it so as not to burn.
3. Once butter is melted, add garlic and cook on a low simmer, stirring often, about 4 to 5 minutes, until garlic is tender.
4. Remove the garlic butter and put in a heat-safe bowl. Put the bowl in the refrigerator until cooled, but not set, about 10 minutes.
5. Remove garlic butter from the refrigerator and add the parsley and the Parmesan cheese. Using a fork, mix well to combine.
6. Cut the baguette in half, then slice lengthwise, leaving the spine intact, so you will have 2 halves split open.
7. Place the bread on the baking sheets and spread 2 tablespoons of the garlic butter mixture onto each side of the bread.

8. Place the baking sheets in the preheated oven on the middle rack and bake for 10 minutes.
9. Then set the oven to broil at 500°F and cook for exactly 2 minutes.
10. Remove the bread from the oven and using a clean hand towel, fold the bread halves together and move to a cutting board.
11. Using the clean hand towel, firmly grasp the hot bread to cut into 2-inch serving size pieces.

STORAGE

- Leftover garlic bread does not reheat well, instead cut it into cubes to create croutons for your next salad. Store croutons at room temperature in a zip-top bag for up to 1 day.
- **For Team Dinner Meal Prep:** Prep the garlic bread through 7, and then wrap the baking sheets tightly with foil. Bring to the host's home, heat oven to 350°F, unwrap the baking sheets and continue with Steps 8-11.

MAKES APPROXIMATELY 14 SERVINGS

NUTRITION INFORMATION PER SERVING—**Calories:** 108 **Carbohydrate:** 10g **Protein:** 2g **Fat:** 7g

APPENDIX

PERSONAL NUTRITION CALCULATIONS

In chapter 2 we discussed the importance of getting the right amounts and the right balance of macronutrients and saw examples of the average amounts young runners are recommended to consume. In this appendix you will get the tools you need to fine-tune your energy intake and hydration even further.

As seen throughout chapter 2, kilograms and grams are commonly used for nutrition calculations. So let's look at how to convert pounds into kilograms.

TABLE A.1. HOW TO CONVERT POUNDS TO KILOGRAMS

Calculation

X pounds ÷ 2.2046 = Z kilograms

Example:

130 pounds ÷ 2.2046 = 58.97 kilograms (59 rounded)

Calculate your own weight in kilograms

pounds:_____ ÷ 2.2046 = _____

A gram measures weight, while a calorie measures energy. Different foods have different calories per gram: fat has more than protein or carbohydrates. Understanding the grams of carbohydrate, protein, and fat in a food allows you to calculate its calorie content. This knowledge can help you manage your energy needs as a runner, ensuring that you are taking in enough energy to match the demands of your growth and development, as well as your running.

TABLE A.2. HOW TO CONVERT MACRONUTRIENT GRAMS TO CALORIES

MACRONUTRIENT	MULTIPLIER	EXAMPLE
Carbohydrate grams	× 4 = calories	30g × 4 = 120 calories
Protein grams	× 4 = calories	20g × 4 = 80 calories
Fat grams	× 9 = calories	10g × 9 = 90 calories

Hydration is the glue that helps provide structural integrity to your building blocks. Without proper hydration, other areas of your body will be compromised and not able to perform optimally when you need them to. Chapters 2 and 3 discussed the tools for how to recognize signs of dehydration and heat stroke, as well as overhydration and how to hydrate around your workouts. You can further develop your knowledge and tools around your specific hydration needs by determining your sweat rate during exercise.

TABLE A.3. HOW TO FINE-TUNE YOUR HYDRATION NEEDS WITH A SWEAT RATE TEST

STEP 1	Plan on a 60-minute workout. Weigh yourself before exercise in a consistent manner. For example, without clothing or with your trainer kit on pre-workout.	Record Weight	Example: 120 pounds
STEP 2	Keep track of how much fluid you consume during your workout.	Record Fluid	Example: 12 ounces
STEP 3	Do not urinate and weigh immediately after exercise in a consistent manner. For example, if you weighed with your trainer kit on, keep it on when you weigh post exercise	Record Weight	Example: 119 pounds
STEP 4	Subtract post-workout weight from pre-workout weight to determine pounds lost.	Record Pounds Lost	Example: 1 pound loss = 16 ounces. This is your sweat rate per hour and what you should strive to consume in future workouts.
STEP 5	Multiply pounds lost × 3 to determine how much fluid to replace post workout	Cups of fluids to replace losses, consumed at a rate of 16 ounces of fluids/hour.	1 × 3 = 3 cups (24 ounces)

HOW TO CREATE YOUR PERSONAL NUTRITION PROFILE

Adopting the average needs of a typical young runner as outlined in chapter 2 is a great place to start in fine-tuning your energy intake. For those who want to fine-tune based on their own unique physiology, you will find formulas for calculating your daily macronutrient energy needs based on weight in "Your Basic Personal Nutrition Profile," below. And for those who want to fine-tune even further, you can incorporate calculations based on sex, height, and level of physical activity in your personal nutrition profile on page 254.

CALCULATING NEEDS BY MACRONUTRIENT

As stated in chapter 2, to better understand how many macronutrients you may need to fuel your body and enhance your running and training properly, the Youth Running Consensus Statement recommends:

Carbohydrate: 6 to 10g/kg/day

Protein: 1.2 to 2.0g/kg/day

Fat: 1.0 to 2.0g/kg/day

YOUR BASIC PERSONAL NUTRITION PROFILE

Example—Young Runner Weighing 130 Pounds

Step 1: Convert your Body Weight in Pounds to Kilograms (kg), as done in table A.1 on the first page of this Appendix.

Body Weight in Pounds ÷ 2.2046 = _____kg

Example:

130 ÷ 2.2046 = 59kg

Step 2: Calculate Needs by Macronutrient

TYPE OF FUEL: CARBOHYDRATE	AMOUNT: 6 TO 10G/KG/DAY
*6 to 10g/kg/day	59g × 6 = 354g of carbohydrate/day to 59g × 10 = 590g of carbohydrate/day
Caloric need (see table A.2 on page 249)	354g × 4 = 1416 calories to 590g × 4 = 2360 calories

TYPE OF FUEL: PROTEIN	AMOUNT 1.2 TO 2.0G/KG/DAY*
*1.2 to 2.0g/kg/day	59 × 1.2 = 71g of protein/day to 59 × 2.0 = 118g of protein/day
Caloric need (see table A.2 on page 249)	71g × 4 = 284 calories to 118g × 4 = 472 calories

TYPE OF FUEL: FAT	AMOUNT: 1.0 TO 2.0G/KG/DAY*
*1.0 to 2.0g/kg/day	59 × 1.0 = 59g of fat/day to 59 × 2.0 = 118g of fat/day
Caloric need (see table A.2 on page 249)	59g × 9 = calories = 531 to 118g × 9 = calories = 1062 calories

Now that you have calculated your energy needs based on your weight, you can get more detailed by taking into consideration your height, sex, resting metabolic rate, and activity level. These additional calculations will provide you with your total daily energy expenditure.

IMPORTANT TERMS AND CALCULATIONS

RESTING METABOLIC RATE (RMR)

The amount of energy you need at rest plus light activities like using the bathroom and going for a walk.

The use of adult-based equations to predict RMR in adolescent athletes is not recommended, as these have been shown to underestimate energy expenditure (by up to 300 calories/day). A recent study resulted in these new predictive resting metabolism equations for adolescents:[69]

RMR [Female]

=11.1 × BM[kg] + 8.4 × height [cm] - 537

RMR [Male]

=11.1 × BM[kg] + 8.4 × height [cm] - 340

69 Desbrow, Ben. "Youth Athlete Development and Nutrition." Sports Medicine 51, no. 1 (September 13, 2021). https://doi.org/10.1007/s40279-021-01534-6.

PHYSICAL ACTIVITY LEVEL (PAL)

PAL is used in combination with the RMR calculation to determine your Total Daily Energy Expenditure (TDEE), the total energy you use in a day.

PHYSICAL ACTIVITY LEVEL (PAL)	CALCULATION
Sedentary (little or no exercise due to injury or illness)	RMR × 1.2 = TDEE
Lightly active (light exercise/sports 1 to 3 days a week)	RMR × 1.375 = TDEE
Moderately active (moderate exercise/sports 3 to 5 days/week)	RMR × 1.55 = TDEE
Very active (hard exercise/sports 6 to 7 days/week)	RMR × 1.725 = TDEE
Extra active (very hard exercise sports & physical job or 2 workouts/day)	RMR × 1.9 = TDEE

PUTTING IT ALL TOGETHER: YOUR DETAILED PERSONAL NUTRITION PROFILE

STEP 1: CONVERT YOUR BODY WEIGHT IN POUNDS TO KILOGRAMS (KG)

Body Weight in Pounds ÷ 2.2046 = _____kg

Example:

130 ÷ 2.2046 = 59kg

STEP 2: CONVERT YOUR HEIGHT IN FEET AND INCHES TO CENTIMETERS (CM)

Calculate your height:

Feet × 12 = ___ inches

____ inches + ____ inches = ____ inches

Total inches × 2.54 = ____ cm

Example:

5′6″

5 × 12 = 60 inches

60 inches + 6 inches = 66 inches

66 × 2.54 = 167.64cm

STEP 3: CALCULATE YOUR RMR

RMR [Female]

= 11.1 × BM[kg] + 8.4 × height [cm] - 537

Example:

11.1 × 59 + 8.4 × 167.64 - 537 = 1526 [RMR]

RMR [Male]

=11.1 × BM[kg] + 8.4 × height [cm] - 340

Example:

11.1 × 59 + 8.4 × 167.64 - 340 = 1723 [RMR]

STEP 4: USING THE PAL CHART, CALCULATE YOUR TOTAL DAILY ENERGY EXPENDITURE (TDEE)

RMR × Activity Level = TDEE

Example:

RMR [Female]

1526 × 1.9 = 2899

Example:

RMR [Male]

1723 × 1.9 = 3274

UNDERSTANDING YOUR TOTAL DAILY ENERGY EXPENDITURE

Now that you have calculated your TDEE, you have a clear idea of the energy intake you need in order to stay strong and healthy. The TDEE values indicate 2899 calories/day for our female example and 3274 calories/day for our male example. Despite how detailed you choose to get in calculating your energy needs, it is important to remain intuitive to how you're feeling throughout the day and during your workouts. Even if you feel like you're doing all the right things, if you are lacking energy, having difficulty concentrating, experiencing disrupted sleep, or experiencing other signs of one of the nutrition challenges discussed in chapter 4, please consult with a medical professional.

REFERENCES

CHAPTER 1

Armento, Aubrey, Marc Heronemus, Daniel D. Truong, and Christine M. Swanson. "Bone Health in Young Athletes: A Narrative Review of the Recent Literature." *Current Osteoporosis Reports* 21, no. 4 (June 8, 2023): 447–58. https://doi.org/10.1007/s11914-023-00796-5.

Coel, Rachel A., George G. A. Pujalte, Andres I. Applewhite, Tracy Zaslow, George Cooper, Angie N. Ton, and Holly J. Benjamin. "Sleep and the Young Athlete." *Sports Health: A Multidisciplinary Approach* 15, no. 4 (July 19, 2022): 194173812211087. https://doi.org/10.1177/19417381221108732.

Desbrow, Ben. "Youth Athlete Development and Nutrition." *Sports Medicine* 51, no. 1 (September 13, 2021). https://doi.org/10.1007/s40279-021-01534-6.

Goolsby, Marci A., and Nicole Boniquit. "Bone Health in Athletes." *Sports Health: A Multidisciplinary Approach* 9, no. 2 (November 30, 2016): 108–17. https://doi.org/10.1177/1941738116677732.

Hecht, Christian, Nicholas Bank, Brian Cook, and R. Justin Mistovich. "Nutritional Recommendations for the Young Athlete: Current Concept Review." *Journal of the Pediatric Orthopaedic Society of North America* 5, no. 1 (February 1, 2023). https://doi.org/10.55275/JPOSNA-2023-599.

Herting, Megan M., and Xiaofang Chu. "Exercise, Cognition, and the Adolescent Brain." *Birth Defects Research* 109, no. 20 (2017): 1672–79. https://doi.org/10.1002/bdr2.1178.

Krabak, Brian J., William O. Roberts, Adam S. Tenforde, Kathryn E. Ackerman, Paolo Emilio Adami, Aaron L. Baggish, Michelle Barrack, et al. "Youth Running Consensus Statement: Minimising Risk of Injury and Illness in Youth Runners." *British Journal of Sports Medicine* 55, no. 6 (October 29, 2020): 305–18. https://doi.org/10.1136/bjsports-2020-102518.

Mandolesi, Laura, Arianna Polverino, Simone Montuori, Francesca Foti, Giampaolo Ferraioli, Pierpaolo Sorrentino, and Giuseppe Sorrentino. "Effects of Physical Exercise on Cognitive Functioning and Wellbeing: Biological and Psychological Benefits." *Frontiers in Psychology* 9, no. 9 (April 27, 2018). https://doi.org/10.3389/fpsyg.2018.00509.

Sale, Craig, and Kirsty Jayne Elliott-Sale. "Nutrition and Athlete Bone Health." *Sports Medicine* 49, no. 2 (November 6, 2019): 139–51. https://doi.org/10.1007/s40279-019-01161-2.

Thiyagarajan, Dhanalakshmi K., Hajira Basit, and Rebecca Jeanmonod. "Physiology, Menstrual Cycle." PubMed. Treasure Island (FL): StatPearls Publishing, 2022. https://www.ncbi.nlm.nih.gov/books/NBK500020.

Tønnessen, Espen, Ida Siobhan Svendsen, Inge Christoffer Olsen, Atle Guttormsen, and Thomas Haugen. "Performance Development in Adolescent Track and Field Athletes according to Age, Sex and Sport Discipline." Edited by Nir Eynon. *PLOS ONE* 10, no. 6 (June 4, 2015): e0129014. https://doi.org/10.1371/journal.pone.0129014.

Warden, Stuart J., Tim Hoenig, Austin M. Sventeckis, Kathryn E. Ackerman, and Adam S. Tenforde. "Not All Bone Overuse Injuries Are Stress Fractures: It Is Time for Updated Terminology." *British Journal of Sports Medicine*, November 14, 2022. https://doi.org/10.1136/bjsports-2022-106112.

Yazawa, Maki. "A Dietitian on the '4 Seasons' to Know for Cycle Syncing." Well+Good, April 27, 2024. https://www.wellandgood.com/menstrual-cycle-foods.

CHAPTER 2

Berg, Erin K. "Performance Nutrition for the Adolescent Athlete." *Clinical Journal of Sport Medicine* 29, no. 5 (September 2019): 345–52. https://doi.org/10.1097/jsm.0000000000000744.

Casa, Douglas J., Samuel N. Cheuvront, Stuart D. Galloway, and Susan M. Shirreffs. "Fluid Needs for Training, Competition, and Recovery in Track-And-Field Athletes." *International Journal of Sport Nutrition and Exercise Metabolism* 29, no. 2 (2019): 175–80. https://doi.org/10.1123/ijsnem.2018-0374.

Das, Jai K., Rehana A. Salam, Kent L. Thornburg, Andrew M. Prentice, Susan Campisi, Zohra S. Lassi, Berthold Koletzko, and Zulfiqar A. Bhutta. "Nutrition in Adolescents: Physiology, Metabolism, and Nutritional Needs." *Annals of the New York Academy of Sciences* 1393, no. 1 (April 24, 2017): 21–33. https://doi.org/10.1111/nyas.13330.

Desbrow, Ben. "Youth Athlete Development and Nutrition." *Sports Medicine* 51, no. 1 (September 13, 2021). https://doi.org/10.1007/s40279-021-01534-6.

Dietaryguidelines.gov. "Home | Dietary Guidelines for Americans," 2020. https://www.dietaryguidelines.gov.

Hecht, Christian, Nicholas Bank, Brian Cook, and R. Justin Mistovich. "Nutritional Recommendations for the Young Athlete: Current Concept Review." *Journal of the Pediatric Orthopaedic Society of North America* 5, no. 1 (February 1, 2023). https://doi.org/10.55275/JPOSNA-2023-599.

Jäger, Ralf. "International Society of Sports Nutrition Position Stand: Protein and Exercise." *Journal of the International Society of Sports Nutrition* 14, no. 1 (June 20, 2017). https://doi.org/10.1186/s12970-017-0177-8.

Krabak, Brian J., William O. Roberts, Adam S. Tenforde, Kathryn E. Ackerman, Paolo Emilio Adami, Aaron L. Baggish, Michelle Barrack, et al. "Youth Running Consensus Statement: Minimising Risk of Injury and Illness in Youth Runners." *British Journal of Sports Medicine* 55, no. 6 (October 29, 2020): 305–18. https://doi.org/10.1136/bjsports-2020-102518.

Linos, Eleni, Elizabeth Keiser, Matthew Kanzler, Kristin L. Sainani, Wayne Lee, Eric Vittinghoff, Mary-Margaret Chren, and Jean Y. Tang. "Sun Protective Behaviors and Vitamin D Levels in the US Population: NHANES 2003–2006." *Cancer Causes & Control* 23, no. 1 (November 2, 2011): 133–40. https://doi.org/10.1007/s10552-011-9862-0.

McDowall, Jill Anne. "Supplement Use by Young Athletes." *Journal of Sports Science & Medicine* 6, no. 3 (2007): 337–42. https://www.ncbi.nlm.nih.gov/pmc/articles/PMC3787284.

Mohr, Alex E., Ralf Jäger, Katie C. Carpenter, Chad M. Kerksick, Martin Purpura, Jeremy R. Townsend, Nicholas P. West, et al. "The Athletic Gut Microbiota." *Journal of the International Society of Sports Nutrition* 17, no. 1 (May 12, 2020). https://doi.org/10.1186/s12970-020-00353-w.

National Institutes of Health. "Office of Dietary Supplements—Iron." nih.gov, August 17, 2023. https://ods.od.nih.gov/factsheets/Iron-Consumer.

National Institutes of Health. "Vitamin D." nih.gov, 2017. https://ods.od.nih.gov/factsheets/VitaminD-Consumer.

Purcell, Laura K. "Sport Nutrition for Young Athletes." *Paediatrics & Child Health* 18, no. 4 (April 18, 2013): 200–205. https://doi.org/10.1093/pch/18.4.200.

Smith, JohnEric W., Megan E. Holmes, and Matthew J. McAllister. "Nutritional Considerations for Performance in Young Athletes." *Journal of Sports Medicine* 2015 (2015): 1–13.

CHAPTER 3

Benardot, Dan. *Advanced Sports Nutrition*. Champaign, IL: Human Kinetics, 2012.

Casa, Douglas J., Samuel N. Cheuvront, Stuart D. Galloway, and Susan M. Shirreffs. "Fluid Needs for Training, Competition, and Recovery in Track-and-Field Athletes." *International Journal of Sport Nutrition and Exercise Metabolism* 29, no. 2 (2019): 175–80. https://doi.org/10.1123/ijsnem.2018-0374.

Judge, Lawrence W., David M. Bellar, Jennifer K. Popp, Bruce W. Craig, Makenzie A. Schoeff, Donald L. Hoover, Brian Fox, Brandon M. Kistler, and Ali M. Al-Nawaiseh. "Hydration to Maximize Performance and Recovery: Knowledge, Attitudes, and Behaviors among Collegiate Track and Field Throwers." *Journal of Human Kinetics* 79, no. 1 (July 10, 2021): 111–22. https://doi.org/10.2478/hukin-2021-0065.

Martinez, Isabel G., Alice S. Mika, Jessica R. Biesiekierski, and Ricardo J. S. Costa. "The Effect of Gut-Training and Feeding-Challenge on Markers of Gastrointestinal Status in Response to Endurance Exercise: A Systematic Literature Review." *Sports Medicine*, April 15, 2023. https://doi.org/10.1007/s40279-023-01841-0.

Purcell, Laura K. "Sport Nutrition for Young Athletes." *Paediatrics & Child Health* 18, no. 4 (April 18, 2013): 200–205. https://doi.org/10.1093/pch/18.4.200.

Jennifer Sacheck and Nicole Schultz, "Optimal Nutrition for Youth Athletes: Food Sources and Fuel Timing," American College of Sports Medicine, acsm.org, 2017, https://www.acsm.org/docs/default-source/nyshsi_resources/resources/nyshsi-optimal-nutrition-for-youth-athletes.pdf.

Sawka, Michael N., Louise M. Burke, E. Randy Eichner, Ronald J. Maughan, Scott J. Montain, and Nina S. Stachenfeld. "American College of Sports Medicine Position Stand. Exercise and Fluid Replacement." *Medicine and Science in Sports and Exercise*, February 1, 2007. https://pubmed.ncbi.nlm.nih.gov/17277604.

Vitale, Kenneth C., Shawn Hueglin, and Elizabeth Broad. "Tart Cherry Juice in Athletes." *Current Sports Medicine Reports* 16, no. 4 (2017): 230–39. https://doi.org/10.1249/jsr.0000000000000385.

CHAPTER 4

Diedrichs, Phillippa, Sharon Haywood, Nadia Craddock, Georgina Pegram, and Kirsty Garbett. "The Confidence Kit: Building Body Confidence in You and the Young People in Your Life." n.d. https://assets.unileversolutions.com/v1/81511615.pdf?disposition=inline.

Jayanthi, Neeru, Courtney Pinkham, Lara Dugas, Brittany Patrick, and Cynthia LaBella. "Sports Specialization in Young Athletes." *Sports Health: A Multidisciplinary Approach* 5, no. 3 (October 25, 2013): 251–57. https://doi.org/10.1177/1941738112464626.

Koulanova, Alyona, Catherine M. Sabiston, Eva Pila, Jennifer Brunet, Benjamin Sylvester, Allison Sandmeyer-Graves, and Drew Maginn. "Ideas for Action: Exploring Strategies to Address Body Image Concerns for Adolescent Girls Involved in Sport." *Psychology of Sport and Exercise* 56 (September 2021): 102017. https://doi.org/10.1016/j.psychsport.2021.102017.

Lundy, Bronwen, Monica K. Torstveit, Thomas B. Stenqvist, Louise M. Burke, Ina Garthe, Gary J. Slater, Christian Ritz, and Anna K. Melin. "Screening for Low Energy Availability in Male Athletes: Attempted Validation of LEAM-Q." *Nutrients*14, no. 9 (April 29, 2022): 1873. https://doi.org/10.3390/nu14091873.

Melin, Anna, Åsa B. Tornberg, Sven Skouby, Jens Faber, Christian Ritz, Anders Sjödin, and Jorunn Sundgot-Borgen. "The LEAF Questionnaire: A Screening Tool for the Identification of Female Athletes at Risk for the Female Athlete Triad." *British Journal of Sports Medicine* 48, no. 7 (February 21, 2014): 540–45. https://doi.org/10.1136/bjsports-2013-093240.

Mountjoy, Margo, Kathryn E. Ackerman, David M. Bailey, Louise M. Burke, Naama Constantini, Anthony C. Hackney, Ida Aliisa Heikura, et al. "2023 International Olympic Committee's (IOC) Consensus Statement on Relative Energy Deficiency in Sport (REDs)." *British Journal of Sports Medicine* 57, no. 17 (September 1, 2023): 1073–97. https://doi.org/10.1136/bjsports-2023-106994.

National Eating Disorders Collaboration. "Body Image." nedc.com.au, 2022. https://nedc.com.au/eating-disorders/eating-disorders-explained/body-image.

Raj, Marc A., Julie A. Creech, and Alan D. Rogol. "Female Athlete Triad." PubMed. Treasure Island (FL): StatPearls Publishing, 2020. https://www.ncbi.nlm.nih.gov/books/NBK430787.

Schmidt, Tara. "What Is Disordered Eating and When Does It Become an Eating Disorder?" Mayo Clinic Press, February 15, 2024. https://mcpress.mayoclinic.org/nutrition-fitness/what-is-disordered-eating-and-when-does-it-become-an-eating-disorder.

Smolak, Linda. "Body Image in Children and Adolescents: Where Do We Go from Here?" *Body Image* 1, no. 1 (January 2004). 15–28. https://doi.org/10.1016/s1740-1445(03)00008-1.

Vries, Dian A. de, Helen G. M. Vossen, and Paulien van der Kolk–van der Boom. "Social Media and Body Dissatisfaction: Investigating the Attenuating Role of Positive Parent–Adolescent Relationships." *Journal of Youth and Adolescence* 48, no. 3 (November 26, 2018): 527–36. https://doi.org/10.1007/s10964-018-0956-9.

Warner, Daisy. "Disordered Eating: Signs, vs. Eating Disorders, and Causes." www.medicalnewstoday.com, September 22, 2023. https://www.medicalnewstoday.com/articles/disordered-eating.

Weigle, Paul E., and Reem M. A. Shafi. "Social Media and Youth Mental Health." *Current Psychiatry Reports* 26 (December 16, 2023). https://doi.org/10.1007/s11920-023-01478-w.

CHAPTER 5

Guest, Ella, Fabio Zucchelli, Bruna Costa, Radhika Bhatia, Emma Halliwell, and Diana Harcourt. "A Systematic Review of Interventions Aiming to Promote Positive Body Image in Children and Adolescents." Body *Image* 42 (September 2022): 58–74. https://doi.org/10.1016/j.bodyim.2022.04.009.

Holden, Shelley L., and Timothy M. Baghurst. "Ten Practical Strategies Coaches Can Use to Promote Nutrition to Their Athletes." *Strategies* 31, no. 6 (November 2, 2018): 34–41. https://doi.org/10.1080/08924562.2018.1515681.

Rizk, Melissa, Lama Mattar, Laurence Kern, Sylvie Berthoz, Jeanne Duclos, Odile Viltart, and Nathalie Godart. "Physical Activity in Eating Disorders: A Systematic Review." *Nutrients* 12, no. 1 (January 9, 2020): 183. https://doi.org/10.3390/nu12010183.

Sánchez-Díaz, Silvia, Javier Yanci, Daniel Castillo, Aaron T. Scanlan, and Javier Raya-González. "Effects of Nutrition Education Interventions in Team Sport Players. A Systematic Review." *Nutrients* 12, no. 12 (November 28, 2020): 3664. https://doi.org/10.3390/nu12123664.

Smolak, Linda. "Body Image in Children and Adolescents: Where Do We Go from Here?" *Body Image* 1, no. 1 (January 2004): 15–28. https://doi.org/10.1016/s1740-1445(03)00008-1.

Weigle, Paul E, and Reem M. A. Shafi. "Social Media and Youth Mental Health." *Current Psychiatry Reports* 26 (December 16, 2023). https://doi.org/10.1007/s11920-023-01478-w.

Yorke, Elisabeth (Lisette), Tara Evans-Atkinson, and Debra K. Katzman. "Shared Language and Communicating with Adolescents and Young Adults with Eating Disorders." *Paediatrics & Child Health* 26, no. 1 (April 17, 2020). https://doi.org/10.1093/pch/pxaa047.

CHAPTER 6

Contento, Isobel R., Sunyna S. Williams, John L. Michela, and Amie B. Franklin. "Understanding the Food Choice Process of Adolescents in the Context of Family and Friends." *Journal of Adolescent Health* 38, no. 5 (May 2006): 575–82. https://doi.org/10.1016/j.jadohealth.2005.05.025.

DeRosa, Bri. "How to Balance Kid Sports and Dinner." The Family Dinner Project, July 25, 2022. https://thefamilydinnerproject.org/blog/how-to-balance-kid-sports-and-family-dinner.

Ducrot, Pauline, Caroline Méjean, Vani Aroumougame, Gladys Ibañez, Benjamin Allès, Emmanuelle Kesse-Guyot, Serge Hercberg, and Sandrine Péneau. "Meal Planning Is Associated with Food Variety, Diet Quality and Body Weight Status in a Large Sample of French Adults." *International Journal of Behavioral Nutrition and Physical Activity* 14, no. 1 (February 2, 2017). https://doi.org/10.1186/s12966-017-0461-7.

Kinsella, Sarah. "Sports Nutrition for Busy Families and Busy Lifestyles." HealthyChildren.org, n.d. https://www.healthychildren.org/English/healthy-living/nutrition/Pages/Sports-Nutrition-for-Busy-Families-and-Busy-Lifestyles.aspx.

Martinsen, Marianne, and Jorunn Sundgot-Borgen. "Higher Prevalence of Eating Disorders among Adolescent Elite Athletes than Controls." *Medicine & Science in Sports & Exercise* 45, no. 6 (June 2013): 1188–97. https://doi.org/10.1249/mss.0b013e318281a939.

Mountjoy, Margo, Jorunn Kaiander, Sundgot-Borgen, Louise M. Burke, Kathryn E. Ackerman, Cheri Blauwet, Naama Constantini, Constance Lebrun, et al. "IOC Consensus Statement on Relative Energy Deficiency in Sport (RED-S): 2018 Update." *British Journal of Sports Medicine* 52, no. 11 (May 17, 2018): 687–97. https://doi.org/10.1136/bjsports-2018-099193.

Psychology Today. "Parenting a Child with an Eating Disorder," 2024. https://www.psychologytoday.com/us/basics/eating-disorders/parenting-a-child-with-an-eating-disorder#how-should-i-prepare-for-a-conversation-about-my-childs-eating-disorder.

Snuggs, Sarah, and Kate Harvey. "Family Mealtimes: A Systematic Umbrella Review of Characteristics, Correlates, Outcomes and Interventions." *Nutrients* 15, no. 13 (January 1, 2023): 2841. https://doi.org/10.3390/nu15132841.

The Nutrition Source. "Meal Prep Guide," October 2, 2020. https://nutritionsource.hsph.harvard.edu/meal-prep.

Yorke, Elisabeth (Lisette), Tara Evans-Atkinson, and Debra K Katzman. "Shared Language and Communicating with Adolescents and Young Adults with Eating Disorders." *Paediatrics & Child Health* 26, no. 1 (April 17, 2020). https://doi.org/10.1093/pch/pxaa047.

Ziegler, Amanda M., Christina M. Kasprzak, Tegan H. Mansouri, Arturo M. Gregory, Rachel A. Barich, Lori A. Hatzinger, Lucia A. Leone, and Jennifer L. Temple. "An Ecological Perspective of Food Choice and

Eating Autonomy among Adolescents." *Frontiers in Psychology* 12 (April 21, 2021). https://doi.org/10.3389/fpsyg.2021.654139.

APPENDIX

Desbrow, Ben. "Youth Athlete Development and Nutrition." *Sports Medicine* 51, no. 1 (September 13, 2021). https://doi.org/10.1007/s40279-021-01534-6.

Mangieri, Heather. "Healthy Hydration for Young Athletes: Ways to Prevent Fluid Loss from Becoming Detrimental." NATA News, July 2018. https://www.nata.org/sites/default/files/healthy-hydration-for-young-athletes.pdf

Reale, Reid J., Timothy J. Roberts, Khalil A. Lee, Justina L. Bonsignore, and Melissa L. Anderson. "Metabolic Rate in Adolescent Athletes: The Development and Validation of New Equations, and Comparison to Previous Models." *International Journal of Sport Nutrition and Exercise Metabolism* 30, no. 4 (July 1, 2020): 249–57. https://doi.org/10.1123/ijsnem.2019-0323.

RECIPE INDEX

ACKNOWLEDGMENTS

My early ideas for this book started nearly ten years ago, going through many iterations before I finally found its purpose and audience. Throughout the journey, I often shared my thoughts with my mom, who battled Parkinson's Disease. Even when I wasn't sure how much she could hear, just weeks before she passed, she surprised me by asking, "How's your book coming along?" "Well, I haven't written it yet, Mom." And honestly, it was very much in the early proposal stage. She looked at me with both a telling and believing face and said, "Well, you will." From then on, I knew I didn't have a choice. Mom believed. I needed to believe, too. Some of my fondest memories are of my dad coaching young runners. His love for the sport and the life lessons he instilled in his athletes were the heartbeat of his work. In his final days, he often reminisced about those coaching years, and I've carried his wisdom with me throughout writing the book. To my daughter Anika—your growth in running was a guiding light for this project. As you forged your own path, my ideas for this book evolved. You believed in me, and I felt that as I wrote. My husband, Joe—thank you for being my rock, and walking alongside me as I navigated the challenging new landscape of writing a book, sending me on writing retreats when I needed it most, and cheering me on when any doubts crept in.

Janine Lange—I am so grateful for you, and your creative spirit. You brought my recipe ideas to life and spearheaded recipe development so that the readers of this book will have only the best nutrition tools to execute the principles laid out. Janine, Colette Lewis, and Amenah Razeghi, your talents in the kitchen shine in the recipes you developed. Many of them will now be staples in our home and many more. And to my recipe testers—Maria Carantit, Kaeli Lange, Anne Jaworski, Mike Simmons, Julie Villaire—your thoughtful approaches to testing recipes only elevated how they appear on the page. Your insights were invaluable. To the P3Running coaches and community—your support and the lessons I learn from you daily fueled my desire to support future generations of runners. Thank you for inspiring me to keep going.

Mariah Woodfield and Ashley Ford—thank you for your assistance with research.

Jordana Tobelem—thank you for helping bring the nutrition curriculum to life. I'm deeply grateful to everyone who has been part of this journey. Lauren Lexa, you gave me my first writing job and have supported me for over 30 years. To my best friend, Julie Hurlbert, your unwavering support and thoughtful feedback were essential to my process. Mary Frasier, thank you for being a sounding board for my countless ideas during our runs through the Issy Alps and for inspiring the Power Breakfast Cookie recipe. Anne Jaworski, my writing partner, from Hugo House to writing retreats, you've been a constant source of support. Maggie Green—your insight when I initially thought this would just be a cookbook was invaluable. Cynthia Nims—your guidance in recipe writing was so helpful. Tim, my brother, thank you for giving me that final nudge to hit "send" on the first draft. And to my Seattle "parents," Nancy and Tom—your belief in me has meant the world. And to all my friends and family for understanding all the rain checks along the way. Lastly, to Kierra and the VeloPress team—thank you for guiding me from proposal to final draft.

ABOUT THE AUTHOR

photo by Adam Haverstock

Michele Pettinger started running at a young age in the Midwest under the tutelage of her father, the high school cross country and track coach. She has a passion for carrying on the legacy of reaching young runners and helping them build a solid nutritional foundation that will empower them now and long into their future running careers. She holds a master's degree in communication studies and had a career as a technical writer before she fell in love with trail running while living in the Pacific Northwest, where she founded P3Running, a collective of coaches specializing in custom run and nutrition coaching.

Michele is an RRCA Level II Certified Running Coach, Certified Specialist in Fitness Nutrition, and Certified Functional Nutrition counselor. She is most at home on the trails, training for ultramarathon distances. Michele lives in Santa Cruz, California, with her husband, Joe. They have a grown daughter, Anika.